The Politics of Development

THE EDWIN O. REISCHAUER LECTURES, 1988

The Politics of Development

PERSPECTIVES ON TWENTIETH-CENTURY ASIA

Robert A. Scalapino

HARVARD UNIVERSITY PRESS
CAMBRIDGE, MASSACHUSETTS
LONDON, ENGLAND
1989

Library of Congress Cataloging-in-Publication Data

Scalapino, Robert A.
  The politics of development.
    "The Edwin O. Reischauer lectures, 1988"—Half-t.p.
   Includes index.
    1. Asia—History—20th century. I. Title.
  II. Title: Edwin O. Reischauer lectures.
DS35.S353 1989   950.4'2   89–11041
ISBN 0–674–68757–4 (alk. paper)

*To those who will lead Asia into
the twenty-first century*

Acknowledgments

I SHOULD LIKE to pay homage to those who have taught me over many decades—my teachers at Santa Barbara and Harvard, including Edwin O. Reischauer, to whom this lecture series is dedicated; my colleagues at Berkeley and elsewhere; and my students, who now stretch back through several generations. From all of these individuals, I have learned and am learning.

Contents

The Politics of Development

I Prelude

ASIA CAME TO the Industrial Revolution late, and for this reason its modern history lies almost wholly within the twentieth century. The very fact that we use terms like "peasant," "artisan," and "merchant" (not "entrepreneur") to describe the primary classes in the early part of this century testifies to the nature of Asian societies and their stage of economic development.

One can argue over whether there was a distinctive Asian mode of production, but it cannot be doubted that until recently most Asian cultures rested on an economic foundation of intensive agriculture. In the political realm, the nation-state did not yet exist, at least in a form recognizable today, and the concept of sovereignty—even that of nationalism—remained for the future. However sophisticated the institutions of governance, moreover, politics in the independent portions of Asia was in essence highly personalized, via some combination of officialdom—civil or military—and a supreme ruler, normally a monarch. Statutes and custom combined to provide guidelines, but basically people were governed by men, not by law. At the village or district level, this generally meant rule by elders for whom tradition set firm perimeters but whose wisdom or lack thereof could be decisive. The social order differed from one society to another, but everywhere a strict hierarchy existed, with vertical relations predominating over horizontal ones.

THIS WAS ASIA as late as the opening years of this century, partial exceptions acknowledged. It is also important to recall that vast parts of Asia were introduced to Westernism via progressive encroachment, which led to subjugation. To provide a balanced assessment of the results of colonial rule, and more particularly its impact upon subsequent socioeconomic and political developments, is not easy. On the one hand, certain of its consequences were disintegrative. Generally it delegitimized old elites, exposing them to their subjects as impotent, or in some cases turning them into cultural hybrids, affected to such an extent by the ways—and language—of the colonializing power that they were in some degree separated from their own people. In certain instances, moreover, imperial policies led to the creation of plural societies, with groups such as Indians and Chinese permitted or encouraged to emigrate to Southeast Asia to undertake functions that the indigenous people shunned.

There was also a tendency to adopt the principle of divide and conquer, a natural political law for any governor. Often this meant cultivating indigenous minorities, singly or in combination, at the expense of indigenous majorities. Sometimes religion was used (though generally not deliberately) as an instrument in this respect. In any case, Christianity—following the earlier paths of Buddhism and Islam—supported pluralism, and hence division, with doctrines that even when blended with a particular culture challenged some of the most fundamental precepts of Asian tradition. As is now commonly recognized, Western missionaries, although they varied greatly in type and effectiveness, were the first modern revolutionary agents to work toward overthrowing the old order in Asia.

On the other hand, colonialism also played an integrative role. Colonial powers took regions composed of diverse ethnic or tribal groups, regions that had previously been only loosely knit together, and imposed upon them an organized government. And through that government, they enforced law and order to a degree and on a scale hitherto unknown. From these developments emerged the nation-state of later times, a state not infrequently burdened with incongruous boundaries and incompatible multiethnic groups but nonetheless sufficiently formed to survive the travails of the post-independence era. Furthermore, while colonial rule did much to delegitimize old elites, it contributed greatly to the training of new elites at least partially equipped to handle the complex problems of independence and interaction with the world at large.

Perhaps it was easier to cultivate a new military elite than to create a new civil elite. Arguably, it required a less profound cultural change to accommodate to Sandhurst or similar Western military schools and to the technology of modern warfare than to other attributes of Western society. It is true that there was a profound difference between, on the one hand, the modes of traditional Asian conflict and the requirements demanded of the earlier warrior and, on the other, the structure, expertise, and behavioral patterns shaping the Western military institutions of the nineteenth century and thereafter. But the more mechanical aspects of accommodation were dictated by the weaponry itself, and the hierarchy, discipline, and sense of professionalism that have marked military modernization could be achieved at least in part by adaptations of the Asian past.

It should be noted that European and American colonizers

generally sought to impress upon the members of the military elite being trained that their purpose was to serve the state, not to rule it. This was in accordance with the values of current Western society, if not wholly with its imperial practices. As we are now aware, the extent to which the new Asian military class adhered to this principle varied greatly; both the circumstances of decolonization and subsequent events were prominent factors in determining the post-independence military role, as I shall later discuss.

Creating a new civilian elite, and more particularly an official class in the image of the Western civil servant, was a more complex task, since in its optimal form this involved imbuing individuals with new values as well as teaching them special skills. Such concepts as considering office holding to be a public trust, applying rules without fear or favor, and abiding by the verdict of the people as expressed through their elected representatives—concepts held in the advanced West, although never fully followed—were for the most part very foreign to traditional Asian officials and, what is more important, to the societies they governed. Nor could Western tutelage be consistent. It was one thing to serve in one's own society, with its accrued rules and customs; it was quite another to rule over a foreign society in which one's legitimacy was basically dependent upon military power, and in which one was judged by standards different from those that applied at home. With regard to officialdom, colonialism thus superimposed ambiguous principles on traditional ones that remained deeply embedded. No fact was so pregnant with implications for the future.

The role of colonialism in implanting basic political values was at least equally inconsistent and paradoxical. The paradox, moreover, grew with time. There was nothing especially contradictory about the initial imposition of authoritarian Western rule on Asian colonies, since authoritarianism in varying degree had long prevailed there. Moreover, Western rule was often indirect, initially allowing indigenous elites and systems to continue functioning. As parliamentarism and other attributes of modern democracy developed in the West, however, the gap between governance at home and rule abroad grew steadily more conspicuous—both to citizens in Europe and to colonials, especially the new elites. In reality, Western imperialism was being undermined politically at an accelerating rate—and by the imperialists themselves. In every institution of higher learning, even in secondary schools, whether in the colony or the "mother country," the basic political theme was democracy. Indeed, wars were being fought in the West ostensibly to save democracy. Yet Asian nationalist movements flying Western-style democratic banners were suppressed in all Asian colonies except the Philippines.

From this evolving paradox stemmed two predictable developments. On the one hand, Asian nationalism in its various manifestations became increasingly radicalized, whether in the form of Gandhi's *satyagraha* or the more martial movements that emerged with the aid of Japan in the final stages of World War II. But what is equally important, Western citizens became increasingly divided over the moral and political issues surrounding imperialism, and their governing elites became increasingly troubled over how to deal with the political challenges to imperial rule.

Despite the devastating effect of two wars within thirty years, the Western European imperial powers could have mustered enough military strength to crush the independence movements of the immediate post-1945 era, although those movements would surely have regrouped and been victorious in the end. But Asian nationalism triumphed over European imperialism at this particular time because of the agonizing self-doubt, the partial rather than total commitment, of even those imperialist nations that chose to fight. To be sure, economic cost was involved, but one should not minimize the fact that the political paradox afflicting Western imperialism had grown too flagrant to survive.

I HAVE MADE only passing mention of the economic factor. It is well known that colonialism in its earlier manifestations derived from, or was handmaiden to, economic interests. Yet in its unfolding, many other factors supported imperial expansion, chief among them the need to build buffers to protect possessions already held. Occasionally, as in the case of the Philippines, a colony was inherited as the unforeseen result of a war fought for other reasons. Yet whatever the motivations prompting it, Western imperialism tended to foster a repetitive economic pattern: raw materials were exported from the colony to advance the industrial base of the imperial power—a vertical division of labor. Economic modernization, therefore, though not absent, was largely confined to advancing this structure. And from this situation there emerged the most important paradox of all: the political system being promoted was that of parliamentary democracy, but the socioeconomic structure being supported was strongly traditional, with only such modifications as fitted imperial interests. A classic example was the Philippines. Surely this was the supreme contradiction with which much of Asia had to wrestle in the early years after World War II.

There are two other contributions of great significance, quite different in nature from the one described above, that the West bequeathed to Asia, both its colonial and noncolonial portions. First was the single most powerful idea transmitted from the West to Asia in the nineteenth century: the idea of progress. Not the endless wheel of life, with everything returning to its point of origin, but ever upward, ever onward—this was the Western message. It is also the idea underlying all modern thought.

Second, by introducing the fruits of science in medicine, imposing relative political stability, and sharing advances in agriculture, the West contributed mightily to the population explosion that was underway in much of Asia by the end of the nineteenth century. The social, economic, and political implications of this development, to be sure, were slow to dawn upon Westerners and Asians alike.

THUS FAR, I have been seeking to highlight particular aspects of the colonial heritage in Asia. But what of the heritage of noncolonial Asia? Here too, as I have already suggested, Western influence was extensive and sustained. Indeed, some might argue that colonialism as such was not the most important variable when one seeks to interrelate politics and economic development. Let us therefore briefly examine salient premodern characteristics of the two important societies of Northeast Asia, China and Japan. It may be objected that China, as many have insisted, was a semi-colony by the late nineteenth century, the preserve not of one but of many imperial powers. Without ignoring the role of various foreign powers in China, I reject the view that imperialism was the controlling or dominant factor in retarding China's development until 1937. I would argue that the Japanese intrusion into China had a decisive influence on all internal developments from that year to the Communist victory in 1949. Prior to 1937, however, the basic problems China faced in adjusting to the world around it and finding an appropriate developmental path lay within China; they were extensively influenced, but not governed, by external factors.

To appreciate this fact, one should look first at Japan, a nation that was to set standards for other Asian countries in maintaining its integrity and pursuing a coherent developmental strategy. Japan's first and most obvious advantages lay in the size of its population and territory at the onset of its modernization drive. In 1868, at the time of the Meiji Restoration, the Japanese population was slightly less than thirty million and very homogeneous. The technology of the times, moreover, ensured that transport and communications could make the Japanese islands a viable entity despite their longitudinal spread. In modern times, we have numerous illustrations of the fact that there is an optimal size for rapid political integration and economic growth. Societies like China and India remain handicapped even now by considerations of territorial size and especially of population.

In contrast to China, moreover, Japan was a corporative society, one with a high degree of vertical integration. Perhaps nothing was more important to the tasks at hand than this. The hierarchical relations within the family were transmitted to relations between the family and the community, and between the community and higher units of society. Japan's so-called centralized feudalism thus became more of an entry point than a barrier to the process of political integration, particularly when the imperial symbol could be restored. In China, the elements of egalitarianism, family centrism, and greatly diverse subcultures were sufficient to inhibit integration. When Sun Yat-sen and others referred to the Chinese people as loose grains of sand, they had these aspects of Chinese culture in mind.

The traditional structure of Chinese governance had taken some account of these factors: officials at the center had been aided by locally based gentry, the private governance of the family had powerfully supplemented external rule, and the imperial institution had served as a symbol of unity while its power had been kept within bounds. Unfortunately for

China, the imperial institution—being in the hands of the Manchu by the time China was brought into the modern stream—was of limited service to the nationalist cause. And when the traditional political structure collapsed, no available external model provided hope of success. The West simply had nothing to offer early twentieth-century China in the form of a political system that could be emulated or adapted. The unfolding of modern China's tragedy is inextricably connected with this fact.

Meanwhile, in Japan the corporate nature of the society enabled early experimentation with complex organization, that indispensable forerunner of twentieth-century development, economic or political. It is enormously important to note that the dominant military class of late Tokugawa Japan, possessed of unchallengeable legitimacy, took advantage of a prolonged period of peace to "civilianize" itself, delving into administrative and entrepreneurial activities involving relatively sophisticated managerial techniques. Without abandoning certain values and modes of behavior associated with their antecedents, military men undertook new roles in the public and private sectors.

It was precisely in this period that the traditional elites of China were undergoing a process of delegitimization and division. This process, more than any other factor, foreshadowed the chaotic period that lay ahead. The Chinese revolution—if this is an appropriate term for the events of the early twentieth century—was caused primarily not by the upsurge of new classes but by deep fissures within the old elites, and by a resulting vacuum of power that could not be adequately filled for many decades. The fact that the traditional military class was strongly Manchu, not Han, and that the emerging military class lacked the status, unity, and experience to govern effectively, precluded the type of transition to a new era subsequently experienced by many late-developing societies and not incompatible with China's own earlier history.

It is appropriate at this point to probe—with care and humility—certain psychological factors applicable to these two societies. In China, the official and intellectual classes had a degree of self-confidence difficult to shake, and to some degree this mind-set characterized the society at large. China, center of civilization, self-sufficient in its vastness, accustomed to dealing with barbarians according to their deserts—did such a people, with such a heritage, have any need for foreign travel, goods, or ideas? This mood, so pervasive a century ago, has not completely disappeared, even today. It has powerfully affected both the timing and the nature of the Chinese response to external stimuli.

To be sure, even in the mid-nineteenth century, there were Chinese with inquiring minds, individuals willing to experiment with foreign gadgets and concepts, and their numbers grew with time. But in the imperial era, most of them were on the periphery of their society, not at its center. And when certain individuals with authority proposed—somewhat unrealistically—that a distinction be made between foreign technology and foreign culture, the purpose was to confront the West, not to join it, and certainly not to transform Chinese society. When the Qing dynasty was finally driven to political reform, it was too late.

Why did Japanese leaders in company with their society turn outward on a broad spectrum of fronts beginning in the early Meiji era, despite recurrent challenges from the anti-foreign purists in their midst? Perhaps they could appreciate the challenge of the West more easily because the lessons of China and southern Asia lay before them. Perhaps also, having relatively firm control of their government and society, they could borrow from abroad with greater assurance of

being able to turn foreign innovations to their advantage. But
it is vitally important that in their tradition lay a lengthy
history of borrowing from others; they accepted the fact that
they existed on the periphery of a great civilization, with yet
another (India) on the distant horizon. The Japanese were
accustomed to being small as well as being special. Consequently, elements of doubt, and hence of need, were mixed
with recurrent waves of arrogance born of the conviction—
powerfully cultivated in modern times—that they were indeed a superior race. It is this paradoxical mixture of self-
doubt and assurance that marks the Japanese psyche and
has contributed so much to Japan's triumphs—and to its
trauma as well.

Implicit in the foregoing remarks is the fact that whatever
problems it posed for flexibility and change, Sinic culture in
its broadest dimensions could make a significant contribution
to Asian development. As Japan so graphically illustrated, it
was not necessary to obliterate the past in order to build the
future. China, Japan, and Korea, for example, shared a respect for education, for the family as the critical nucleus of
society and repository of values, and for a pervasive work
ethic—all of which could support developmental goals under
certain conditions. As indicated, these traits were first har-
nessed to the new tasks at hand by the Japanese, not only for
themselves but for the Koreans and those Chinese who came
under their governance. Indeed, certain observers, noting
conditions in Taiwan and Manchuria in the early 1930s—as
well as in Hong Kong and Singapore—asserted that the Chinese were marvelous entrepreneurs and agriculturalists if
someone else governed them. In reality, the formidable problem of scale, the less supportive aspects of Sinic culture all
too apparent in its home environment, and the cumulative
recent experiences combined to provide the dismal picture of early twentieth-century China. Even now, as our cen-

tury draws to a close, after momentous efforts to make China governable and a much greater array of developmental experiences, certain old problems persist, with new ones added, as we shall see. But by the same token, each of the four so-called Small Dragons—namely, South Korea, Hong Kong, Taiwan, and Singapore—have drawn deeply upon the benefits available from the Sinic culture which they share, though the fact that their policies have been tuned to take maximum advantage of their cultural assets represents an equally important factor.

IT IS TO BE hoped that we will grow beyond all forms of reductionism in analyzing basic social phenomena. Cultural determinism is no more acceptable than economic determinism or than a form of political determinism currently in vogue which can be labeled "policy determinism"—namely, the thesis that policies are the sole important variable. Our challenge is to handle complexity, including the changing relative importance of multiple variables as both a given society and the global context in which it exists undergo successive alterations. Thus, in dealing with the evolution of modern Asia, one must determine the precise mix of culture, experience, scale, timing, leadership, and policy that shapes the contours of a given society at a given point in time and determines the perimeters within which alternative courses can be pursued. Such a formulation is unacceptable to those who want to find the key to social evolution in the permanent dominance of a single variable, in the discovery of a holistic immutable truth. Unfortunately, perhaps, such a "truth" does not exist, as the course of human events in the twentieth century makes indisputably clear. Truth lies in achieving as close an approximation as possible of the shifting mosaic of causative factors that in combination explain and account for the most basic societal trends. Theory, whether abstract or specific, must be constructed by building upon this approach.

In this context, let me briefly examine those events in the two decades prior to the end of World War II that were to set the stage for the emergence of a new Asia after 1945. In the broadest sense, we can look upon this era as one in which nationalism in diverse forms was on an upward curve. In Europe, the problems unresolved or created by the First World War led those who felt cheated to redouble their efforts to alter the regional and global distribution of power. Employing the potent appeals of race and culture, demanding organic unity from those they governed, and raising mobilization techniques to new levels of effectiveness, first the Italian Fascists and then the German Nazis sought to play upon grievances and take advantage of the economic-political malaise that accompanied the postwar years. Theirs was a call to arms, figuratively and literally, in an effort to revitalize a dispirited and divided people.

Nationalism in the United States took a different form. Once again, America turned inward after a brief, intensive foray into European politics. "Old-world ills" rekindled American contempt for Europe and a renewed belief in U.S. self-sufficiency. Resentment at being unappreciated was coupled with a feeling of defilement. How could one maintain purity unless one stood aloof from European intrigue and from the endless balance-of-power games that seemed largely devoid of moral principle? And why did a rising power like the United States need the quarrelsome, selfish states whose prime had passed? Thus, America's nationalism was represented by its reversion to pride in being at once different and superior in moral as well as material terms. The Great Depression soon served as a powerful reinforcement of aloofness. Yet the estrangement from Europe stemmed from more than economic causes. The new political tides running on the European continent were neither consonant with American culture nor necessary to secure political support from the American people. To be sure, some citizens, such as the Negroes (as African-Americans were then called) were partly excluded from the American dream; but for a strong majority of Americans, there were few barriers that firm goals and hard work could not overcome. Core values were epitomized by the Fourth of July, the Sunday church service, Thanksgiving, and Christmas. And Irving Berlin, with the help of Kate Smith, summed it all up in "God Bless America."

IF NATIONALISM was on the march throughout much of the West, it was also finding new forms of expression in Asia. In the colonies, young elites were being politicized, and various associations, parties, and secret societies were being organized to arouse the masses at the first step in national liberation. The principal appeals were the call to reclaim one's cultural identity and the demand for economic and political justice, two themes that were not truly compatible but that each contained considerable potency. The quest for cultural identity was championed through various means—religion and language being the most prominent. It is difficult to capture this struggle in all of its complexity. The great mass of peasants had not departed greatly from their traditions. Thus, a significant number of them could be enlisted on behalf of a new cause by means of old values still held dear. Yet whatever the label attached, theirs was a "reactionary" stance in the generic sense of the word. They could be dissuaded from a preference for the ways of their ancestors only with great difficulty. Their satisfaction with that which was and always had been broke the hearts of many who espoused rapid, radical change.

The perspective of the literate, politically motivated members of colonial societies was naturally different. Theirs was the task of defining their identity and then advancing it as a political cause through an intricate combination of old and new values reflecting indigenous forces and external influences. Pain and resentment vied with intellectual excitement and admiration, as the lifestyle and values spawned by Western science and technology entered into their society and personal lives. To wrestle with these conflicting currents was the fate of all those intellectuals and leaders who came on the political stage in colonial Asia during the interwar years.

In the fusion of psychology and politics, the issue of race was omnipresent. Submerged or overt, the Asian's consciousness of white domination of the world—including his own society and to some degree himself—could never be erased. "Why was this so, and why did it have to be?" was the recurrent question throughout Asia. It was taught that there had been a time when the cultures of the yellow and brown races were more advanced than those of the fur-clad barbarians of Europe. (Spokesmen for the yellow race sometimes went further, proclaiming that their race was superior to the brown and black, and in competition with the white race for supremacy.)

Racial pride and ethnic consciousness have always been pronounced in Asia, running the gamut from simple, unadorned xenophobia to sophisticated efforts to take from other cultures and races the instruments necessary to reassert a "rightful superiority." As implied, however, the racial-ethnic factor has figured prominently in intra-Asian (including intrastate) relations, as well as those with the external world; and naturally, racial and cultural identity were generally interwoven. Indeed, the line traditionally drawn by the Chinese between barbarians and civilized people (those accepting Chinese culture) modified (but did not eliminate)

Chinese racism. It should also be acknowledged that racial identification—and the quest for liberation from white dominance—did not preclude a protracted struggle between the two foremost representatives of the yellow race from the late nineteenth century onward. In the contest between cooperation and conflict, moreover, the latter triumphed, as Japanese aggression against China reached its climax with the Pacific War.

If the drive for cultural identity relied heavily upon indigenous supports, the demand for political and economic justice in colonial Asia drew principally upon the avant-garde practices and theories of the Western democracies, modified or challenged in some instances by Marxism-Leninism, which was even more avant-garde. Despite certain efforts to romanticize the past, resulting in the discovery of a Golden Age in traditional Asia, there was little in the Asian tradition that paid homage to a strong, centralized state, popular sovereignty, or egalitarianism. It is true, however, that certain hoary traditions projected a different notion of justice and virtue into the twentieth century, one that continued to compete with modern Western-derived political values. According to this notion, the just ruler was seen as a father who both set an example for his progeny and listened to their complaints; decision making involved consensus rather than majoritarianism; limits on the power of the ruler were imposed by custom rather than law; and there was a strong element of local self-governance. Once again, inner satisfaction—and societal peace—were likely only if some synthesis could be achieved between traditions still expressing the proclivities of the society and the external stimuli that seemed to presage the future.

Many of the issues surrounding the emergence of nationalism in colonial Asia were also present in the two most significant independent Asian states. Let us examine broad trends in China first. For this society, the post-Versailles years constituted a time of troubles. Too vast in area and population to be easily unified with available techniques, China suffered grievously from unending civil strife. Multiple governments ruled portions of the land, their legitimacy resting on little more than military power. The struggle for unification resulted in the militarization of politics, as was subsequently seen in both the Nationalist and Communist ranks. The great losers in Chinese politics of the 1920s and thereafter were the civilians of all political persuasions. But could military governance achieve what civilian rule could not? Could the Kuomintang under Chiang Kai-shek, having gained precarious control over most of China in 1928, bring about sufficient stability to tackle seriously the next task, that of laying the foundations for the nation's sustained development?

For a brief time, the outlook seemed promising. Patriotism and an acceptable ideology provided a potential basis for nation building. Steadily, from the May Fourth movement of 1919 onward, students and other urbanites marched, demonstrated, and wrote fiery polemics against the intrusions of Japan and the European powers. The nationalist movement was at last acquiring a firm base among China's articulate citizenry, one landmark being the huge demonstrations throughout eastern China that followed the incident of May 30, 1925, when British-directed police shot a number of Shanghai youths. Meanwhile, Sun Yat-sen, the indefatigable champion of a modern Chinese nation, loomed larger in death than he had in life. Although he passed away in early 1925, his Three People's Principles—nationalism, democracy, and a concern for the people's livelihood—constituted the creed by which the Nationalists sought to mobilize the Chinese people.

Under these banners, the reunification of China got underway. After 1928 most provinces paid homage, at least nominally, to the national government. The warlordism of earlier years was subdued if not eliminated. Reflecting this fact, the Kuomintang's organizational capacities and internal cohesion improved, and rivals—including the Communists—though not wholly eliminated, were reduced to impotence. On the political front, it seemed possible that China would achieve a unity at least equal to that of the late imperial era, and gradually develop political institutions based upon that dominant party system destined to be prevalent in post-1945 Asia. Economic advances were also registered, in part the product of greater domestic tranquillity, but equally a result of a growing number of scientists, technicians, managers, and skilled workers.

Chiang Kai-shek, who led the nation during these years, could have done more to promote unification and development if in addition to his patriotism, intensity, and steadfastness of purpose he had had greater magnanimity, breadth of vision, and the ability to reach out to those who had skills essential to the tasks at hand. But it is unlikely that any man or group could have remolded China, or even made a decisive start in that direction, in the few years between the conclusion of the Northern Expedition and the second major Japanese attack on China in 1937.

Knowing the serious weaknesses of his country and still giving priority to the liquidation of the Communists, Chiang sought to avoid or postpone conflict with Japan, but events both at home and abroad conspired against his efforts. As a result of Chiang's detention in Xian in December 1936 by elements favoring an end to China's civil strife, a precarious entente was established between Nationalists and Communists, heightening Japanese concerns. The Japanese militarists, now rising to power at home, plunged deeper into China in the summer of 1937, committed to a course that paradoxically gave the Chinese Communists, designated as their most hated foes, the opportunity to seize power. It was entirely understandable that, after the Pacific War had ended, when a group of Japanese generals were visiting Beijing, Mao Zedong interrupted their apologies with the comment, "Gentlemen, we owe our victory to you!"

To understand the facts underlying Mao's words, one must recall China's condition after the renewed Japanese invasion. The war years found the nation once again deeply divided. The more affluent and modern portions, including virtually the entire eastern seaboard, were under Japanese occupation, and the collaborationist Wang Jingwei government—along with its sizable army—was functioning under Japanese authority. Although relations between the Wang government and Tokyo were more complex than has yet been revealed, eastern China, with the exception of certain guerrilla enclaves, was denied to the Nationalists for seven crucial years. In the northwest, meanwhile, the Chinese Communists were combining guerrilla warfare with the politics of inclusion— termed New Democracy—to expand their authority from a few tens of thousands to several millions of adherents, including steadily growing armies. In their territory also, Nationalist authority was barred except in guerrilla areas, and as the Communists took the opportunity to expand their control in the name of the Anti-Japanese War, the Nationalist-Communist struggles both for territory and for supporters threatened to overshadow the campaign against the Japanese.

Thus, the Nationalists, confined largely to interior China, were separated for years from the great majority of the Chinese population. When the Pacific War ended, the tasks confronting them were massive, multiple, and interrelated: they needed to pursue economic, political, and military policies that would restore their legitimacy; to rebuild an institutional structure that had decayed; to revitalize a tired and divided elite that had lost its way; and to find means of communicating with a populace cynical about politics and weary of war. The odds were stacked sharply against success.

Japanese nationalism and the evolution of the Japanese state in the early twentieth century took a strikingly different course from the one followed in China. Japan's central problem stemmed from success, not failure. No other non-Western nation—and few Western nations—had achieved such unity and development as occurred in the decades after the Meiji Restoration. Japan's emulation of the advanced West extended to politics as well as economics. There were flaws in the Meiji constitution—flaws subsequently exploited by the military—but the democracy that emerged in early twentieth-century Japan, subsequently labeled Taisho Democracy, was genuine. Replete with Japanese characteristics, it nevertheless embodied two indispensable requirements: political choice and civil rights. In comparison with other industrializing societies of that era, Japan could correctly be put in the category of democratic states, despite its corporatist features.

In the economic realm also, Japan's progress was spectacular. Early state-sponsored industrial initiatives were largely turned over to the private sector, but with continuing government support. Mercantilism may have come late to Japan, but it was nonetheless potent. And in economics as in politics, the Japanese genius lay in oligarchy. A few large-scale diversified companies possessed resources sufficient for research and development and, at the same time, incentives for competition that encouraged maximum efficiency. The extensive subcontracting system enabled myriad small and medium-sized industries to flourish and to gradually increase their productivity. Underwriting the economy, a strong primary educational system produced a skilled labor force, building a work ethic into the social structure. Moreover,

Japanese workers tended to accept a paternalist system with minimal complaint. Hence, labor strife was rare. At the top, meanwhile, Japan's universities were shaping an economic as well as political elite, with the premium placed upon a general education; managerial training was largely a responsibility of the company into which the college graduate entered and to which he made a lifetime commitment. Finally, the ability to obtain technology from abroad and integrate it successfully into the Japanese system was a striking aspect of Japan's rapid march toward modernity, a product of the cultural attributes earlier noted.

Japan's successes were not merely domestic. They were also displayed in a series of almost unbroken military victories abroad. Only in Siberia did the Japanese fail to accomplish their objectives when they chose to use force. Thus, military exploits earned the nation an empire at relatively limited costs; moreover, this empire was extensively integrated into the primary Japanese economy, thereby contributing in major degree to its expansion. Politics was equally affected. Given its successes, the prestige of the military steadily rose. It came close to being politically invulnerable. The defense of empire, moreover, required a formidable military force, deeply rooted in rural Japan. Gradually, two opposing elements emerged within Japanese society, each seeking to control the course of the nation: an urban, liberal, broadly nationalist, cosmopolitan, civilian elite on the one hand, and a rural, narrowly nationalist, authoritarian, provincial, militarist elite on the other hand. To be sure, there were hybrids and complex shadings, but fundamentally these were the divisions.

The radicals in the militarist group wanted to overthrow not only Western imperialism but the economic system, including their own "corrupt and venal capitalists." Despite certain critical differences and the deep hostility marking their relationship, it is easy to see the spiritual link between this group and the Chinese Communists, with respect to policies as well as antecedents. In the case of both groups, it might be said that the countryside was striking back at the cities, that traditionalism—even if in new garb—was reacting against "over-Westernization," especially in its liberal vein. Certainly, the results were different. The radicals were defeated in Japan, though a portion of their values and a smaller part of their program were continued by a coalition of more conservative militarists and civilian bureaucrats. But even this latter group felt strongly that Japan had a dual mission: to purify itself at home, restoring many of the traditional values that were in danger of being corrupted, and to liberate Asia from the control of the West, enabling the emergence of a Greater East Asian Coprosperity Sphere.

WHILE NATIONALISM in diverse forms was displaying strength both in Asia and in the West in the years after World War I, the first hesitant steps toward institution building at the regional and international levels were also being taken. The principal monument to those efforts was the League of Nations. From the outset, however, the League labored under multiple difficulties. The lack of coherent leadership was a major problem. The United States was not prepared to play the international role that accorded with its newly achieved economic and political strength. Thus, Woodrow Wilson's hope that America would accept global leadership remained a dream. After a bitter struggle between the president and certain powerful senators, the U.S. government chose to stand aloof from the League. As noted earlier, the powerful emotional appeal of self-reliance and noninvolvement in "old-world quarrels" emerged victorious over a sense of responsibility for a stable global order.

Perhaps the effort to create a viable international structure was premature. Much of the world still possessed colonial status. The current capacity of Europe—itself deeply divided—or any of its separate nations either to underwrite the status quo or to take the initiative in creating a new order was exceedingly doubtful. And given America's heritage of isolation, such a venture was too bold. Moreover, the time and patience required would have run counter to the proclivities of U.S. foreign policy: make a total commitment when circumstances seemed to require it, finish the task quickly, and then get out. Thus, an old order based strictly on balance-of-power principles was fading, yet a viable new order could not be produced.

Regional developments in the Pacific-Asian area reflected global conditions. Feeling some guilt over its abandonment of the League and eager to demonstrate its increasing interest in Asia, the Harding administration sponsored the 1921–1922 Washington Conference, bringing Japan and China together with the major Western powers having a stake in the region. The most significant outcome of this conference was the substitution of the five-power and nine-power agreements for the Anglo-Japanese alliance, a pact that had provided a type of regional order for two decades. The thrust was to replace a powerful duumvirate with a collective agreement that spread responsibility more widely. Yet as events were to show, collective responsibility is a dubious principle upon which to rest an international order, if perceptions of national interests increasingly diverge and if meaningful collective sanctions against transgressors are impossible to implement.

Thus, both at the global and regional levels, the type of hegemonic authority exercised earlier by Great Britain was currently impossible because of a lack of either means or will, but efforts to establish collective responsibility were doomed by the circumstances of the times. In a manner reflecting its political culture, the United States continued to espouse policies based on moral suasion. The great hallmark of this era was the Kellogg-Briand Peace Pact of 1928, whereby all nations agreed to outlaw war as an instrument of foreign policy. But in this very period, conflicts of interest were mounting, soon to be exacerbated by the Great Depression.

THE BREAKDOWN IN the international order was at once symbolized and caused by powerful new ideologies and revolutionary movements challenging the classic capitalist democratic system. Nowhere was the challenge sharper than in Asia. Having begun to despair of transferring Western economic and political policies successfully to their societies, a growing number of Asians awoke to the possibility that there were other, more serviceable models which could foster greater political unity and more rapid economic development.

The Russian Revolution made a profound impression on many Asian intellectuals—first and foremost, as a technique of successful revolution, and, second, as the means by which a backward society could take a great leap forward. Marxism in its Leninist form and, shortly thereafter, Fascism as it was propagated by Italy and Germany were both designed to appeal to those in a hurry. Leninism blended an idealistic internationalism with a tough-minded manipulation of nationalism and, in the process, demonstrated how a combination of ideas and sophisticated organizational techniques could be used to rapidly create a mass movement under elitist tutelage. By such means, could not the most intractable ancient regime be toppled? Leninism also offered the opportunity for the new youthful elites of Asia to push seniority aside and become leaders. It promised a way to activate individuals and classes that had previously been only on the outer edge of the political arena, and, having activated them, use them as the foundation of permanent power. Many people believed that the Soviet Union not only represented a "New Democracy" but also that, in contrast to the old democracies, it appeared to be supportive of the national aspirations of colonial and quasi-colonial Asia.

Fascism made some of the same appeals, albeit with certain differences in emphasis. It, too, promised the eradication of old privileged classes and the creation of a socialist society, although this was to be national socialism, with the nation-state the central actor. It, too, made the masses the indispensable base of political power, and advanced organizational and indoctrinational techniques to new levels of effectiveness. In these respects, there was much that united Communism and Fascism despite their bitter enmity. Indeed, it might be said that their enmity was intense partly because they were fighting on the same turf, with similar appeals for legitimacy, for the same clientele. To be sure, there were important differences. Fascism made a nationalist appeal that was far more overt and that was clothed in the raiment of racial superiority. It transferred the concept of class from the nation to the world, playing upon the existing global inequities and proclaiming that legitimate rights were being denied to people who were manifestly superior. Class, for the Fascists, was essentially based upon race and culture. In military conflict, moreover, one's inner qualities were put to the test. Patriotism, sacrifice, the abandonment of egoism for the national good—the traits that, to the Fascists, made a people truly great—were accentuated in time of war.

In diverse ways, Communism and Fascism each had its appeal to various elites in Asia, as I have suggested. The concept of tutelage, undertaken by a vanguard elite central to both doctrines, accorded with the dominant stream of Asian thought. Sun Yat-sen, drawing on tradition, had pioneered such a concept in modern China, and under the Kuomintang it had been built into the principle of one-party guidance, a tutelage that would lead to constitutional democracy at some point in the future, but that meanwhile justified authoritarian rule. In Japan, the concept of tutelage was expanded to encompass the idea that Japan was destined to assist Asia in reaching those goals of independence and development already achieved by the Japanese. This was regional tutelage.

Moreover, for societies that had never valued individualism highly, Leninism and Fascism pledged the sublimation of individual selfishness on behalf of the collective good, whether of the community, the nation, or the world. By the same token, those who saw in capitalism the evils of exploitation and the corrupt values of a hedonistic West could find in either of these doctrines a commitment to a higher purpose. And one should not overlook the power of a racial doctrine, which is always certain to attract adherents.

In essence, the times were ripe for ideological appeals in Asia that contested the classical liberal model previously offered by the West. Meanwhile, on the broader stage, the combined effects of domestic problems and of the anarchic international environment guaranteed that heightened turbulence would afflict much of Asia in the years prior to the outbreak of the Second World War. In virtually every part of the region, protesters were mounting challenges against the prevailing economic and political order. The Pacific War struck the final blow.

As I noted earlier, Japan played a major role in fostering the independence of colonial Asia, even at a time when its defeat guaranteed the liberation of its own imperial possessions. The military and political elites in South and Southeast Asia that were to emerge after August 1945 owed much to Japan, both because it had humiliated their foreign rulers and because it had given them a chance to organize, and in some cases, to arm. In the process, to be sure, Japan had gravely damaged its own image by engaging in excesses of various sorts, and this would be uppermost in the memories of other peoples. But the war had fateful consequences for every part of Asia. In the space of a few years, colonial structures that had extended back as far as three centuries dissolved. Meanwhile, the path to Communist victory in China was cleared, with a new stage in the Chinese revolution soon to be set in motion. And Japan itself was shortly to be purified, though not in the manner that its military men would have preferred. Thus, while many indigenous factors remained to influence the future, the obstacles to change in Asia were less potent in 1945 than at any time in history. A dramatically different era was at hand.

2 | The Struggle to Emerge

THE FIRST TASK IN ASIA after 1945 was to achieve political coherence. To this end, there was only one route: a nation-state had to be created or reconstructed. At the end of the war, Asia was virtually stateless. With few exceptions, however, Asian elites now accepted the validity of Western concepts like sovereignty and the centrality of a nation to any political order. The question was how best to accomplish their political goals. Would negotiation at home and abroad suffice, or would it be necessary to resort to force? Could one use Western liberalism as an ideological appeal and institutional base, or was this doctrine too soft and too prone to divisiveness to overcome the obstacles at hand? And what attitudes should one adopt toward those major powers that seemed eager to shape the world in their image? Alliance, alignment, or aloofness—which was the most appropriate course?

FOR COLONIAL ASIA, the initial answers to these questions were strongly influenced by a combination of recent history and the policies being pursued by the old governors who had returned to their colonies. Therefore, let us first examine the diverse experiences involved in decolonialization. Japan's ability to shape colonial policies had of course vanished with its defeat, although no one can doubt that Japanese rule left a powerful legacy in Korea and Taiwan. The surviving colonial powers were Great Britain, the Netherlands, France, and the United States.

Great Britain negotiated rather than fought its way out of post-1945 Asia, primarily because Winston Churchill and his government were turned out of office soon after the war. Consequently, the transition to independence was relatively orderly. Even the massive disorder on the Indian subcontinent lasted only a short time. Power was given to individuals or coalitions that had acquired legitimacy through previous service in the nationalist movement, personal ties with traditional elites, or both. Since it had not been necessary to fight for independence, the military were rarely more than members of a coalition, and generally not the most significant members. Whatever the indigenous factors lending their weight in other directions, the circumstances of decolonialization themselves were conducive to civilian, liberal governance in the British mold. Parliamentarism was the initial commitment in almost every society formerly under British rule.

The Netherlands abandoned control of the East Indies only with great reluctance, negotiating their departure after a combination of frustrating military operations and mounting external pressures. As a result, the Indonesian nationalist movement contained a sizable military component. Conflict with the Dutch, however, was not protracted, and the Indonesian independence movement was led by civilians whom the Japanese had supported in the final stages of the war. Yet the unification of Indonesia was to prove a formidable task. Stretching some three thousand miles from the Indian Ocean into the South Pacific, possessing myriad subcultures, and at the outset lacking even a common language, Indonesia was more a vision than a reality in the initial years of independence. Thus, the Western political model was bound to be severely tested, and the military soon acquired increased authority in response to internal threats and external ambitions.

Charles de Gaulle, like Winston Churchill, had no intention of dismantling an empire built over several centuries. He and other French leaders hoped to create a French Union that would preserve the ties connecting France and its colonies by reinforcing them with a more flexible institutional framework. The costs of this gamble were to be high for France and for others. It can never be proved that more prescient French policies in the years after 1945 would have produced a different political result in Vietnam. The recent political history of that country had been a tortured one. In the years following 1945, however, few of France's actions supported a viable, moderate Vietnamese leadership.

The United States alone had encouraged a legal nationalist movement in the Asian territory it occupied. Indeed, it had established a timetable for independence in the prewar Philippines. Thus, this people had already had experience with open political organization, competitive elections, and a wide arena of political freedom. The issues lay elsewhere—in the social and economic realms. The tragedy of American rule lay in the fact that its political guidance was not accompanied by the basic economic and social reforms necessary to give democracy adequate foundations.

It should be reiterated that despite the latent appeal of more cohesive ideologies, colonial Asia, with the exception of the French colonies, was initially prepared to accept the Western liberal model as it ventured into independence. Western tutelage had made a deep impact, albeit primarily on the new elites who were assuming the mantle of power. In the schools, on the streets, in the prisons, and even on the battlefield, they had fought for freedom and political representation. They were students, directly or indirectly, of Harold Laski and a host of other Western "progressives." Thus, they often combined their liberalism with socialism, and virtually without exception they expected the state to play an extensive role in the economy as in other facets of the society. But they were not Leninists. They may have been influenced by Marx, but they also knew about the French Revolution, the American Declaration of Independence, and a host of other events in Western history.

Writ large, the diverse colonial legacies revealed as much about the nature of the dominant power as about the cultures of those under their rule. The Japanese had sought to integrate their possessions into the Greater Japan. Nothing was to be omitted or left to chance—language, education, economic system, political institutions. Thus, Japanese was the sole official language and indeed the compulsory medium of all instruction. Primary education was widely dispensed, providing a literate workforce, and the economic system, particularly its industrial component, was expanded, paralleling that of Japan at a lower level. The political system was not replicated but Koreans and Taiwanese were subjects of the emperor, under the same obligations as their Japanese counterparts, though not granted the same rights. It was hardly for lack of effort that Japanese colonial policy did not fully succeed in stripping its colonies of their separate identities.

The British, in contrast, managed to transmit their political values without transmitting their culture in its more extended dimensions, except to a handful of individuals, principally in the upper strata. British aloofness combined with a strong sense of class and ethnic distinction to keep the colonies separate from the ruling nation, socially as well as economically. Integration was never remotely considered, though all colonies were in a special sense wards of the Crown, and this relationship formed a basis for the subsequent British Commonwealth.

In distinction, the French managed to transmit much of their culture without implanting their political values. Perhaps the latter fact reflects the uncertainties surrounding French politics at home, the fact that the French Revolution had never been fully consummated. Ambivalent about politics but secure in their way of life, French colonists dispensed language, cuisine, art, and literature. Uninhibited by the taboos that accompany a strong sense of hierarchy or ethnicity, the French left behind them a significant number of individuals torn between the politics of estrangement and the yearning for cultural compatibility.

The influence of the Dutch was closer to that of the French, but less deep, perhaps reflecting the vastness of the East Indies and its heterogeneous nature, in comparison with the slender resources—human and material—that the Netherlands could expend on its colonies.

To an even greater extent than the British did in their colonies, the Americans bequeathed their political values and institutions to the Philippines, despite the significant cultural disparities. They also transmitted much of their culture, notwithstanding the substantial differences between American egalitarianism and the steep social-political hierarchy characterizing Philippine society.

IN SURVEYING the propensities of the new Asian states, one must acknowledge the vital importance of culture, historical experience, stage of development, and geopolitics as these related to the timing of the nations' emergence into the world stream. Yet the significance of the personal element, often minimized by those who search for the iron laws of development, must not be overlooked. Granting the influences upon leadership exercised by culture, history, and so forth, the character and capacities of individual leaders constituted yet another, extremely important variable. Naturally, the personalities and preferences of these leaders were influenced by such intimate matters as familial relations, childhood experiences, and educational/training opportunities, including ideas acquired from teachers, associates, and spouses. It is precisely here that the psychoanalytic approach has merit, especially if one is prepared to carry it beyond childhood, through life.

And who can doubt that those individuals who come to power after a revolution or at the onset of a new era have a unique opportunity? First-generation leaders can innovate to an extent that is usually impossible for those who follow. They have the chance to set a new course and to establish a new legacy, albeit one that cannot be divorced from the culture in which they operate. They can try many new things, and in the successes and failures of these initial ventures, a record is compiled that establishes perimeters within which future actions are likely to take place, tables of probability for those who follow.

One must not neglect the other side of the coin. At the beginning of a new order, the force of old traditions remains exceedingly powerful, regardless of the destructive actions and bold rhetoric of those aiming at future goals. Moreover, the formal political institutions engendered are perforce weak, since their roots are shallow. Rule is highly personalized, in accordance with the deepest cultural traits of the society. In this setting, first-generation leaders are above all responsible for mobilizing their people around new values and new modes of behavior conducive to an expanded sense of community. They must manipulate nationalist symbols to this end, realizing that nationalism in its more sophisticated forms has in the past appealed essentially only to elites. At the grassroots, xenophobia is exhibited not merely toward those who come from afar but toward all who live beyond the village perimeter.

As noted earlier, an effective appeal—subtle or overt—can often be made on the basis of race, ethnicity, or religion. It is much more difficult, however, to implant in a citizen's mind and heart the loftier vision of the nation-state as a diverse community representing a political order that aims at the common good. Thus, the role of nationalism in committing the masses to the state can easily be exaggerated. Yet it is difficult to overestimate the role that the "Fathers" of their country play as they seek to tutor their people, providing through some combination of coercion and persuasion an order within which development on a new and expanded scale can take place. Their personal values, their political style, their intellectual qualities, and their capacity to understand the times in which their society is living are variables of great importance.

What was the nature of the first-generation leaders of ex-colonial Asia, and what legacies did they bequeath? One might well begin with the Father of modern India. Mahatma Gandhi was to be revered as a saint by millions, but to the British who dealt with him, he was a shrewd politician whose tactics accorded exceedingly well with the vulnerabilities of the British when they played authoritarian roles. Against what other people would nonviolence have worked so well? Gandhi, moreover, identified closely with rural India—Mother India, as it was lovingly called. He was at once sophisticated and simple, well versed in the strategies of mass movements but wary of emphasizing an urban technological revolution. His insistence that rural India be accorded priority has more merit than is commonly acknowledged, though his method of projecting this concept can easily be criticized.

Most first-generation builders instinctively ignored the hinterlands and the need to provide them with modern components, industrial as well as agricultural.

Gandhi was succeeded by another gifted man, Jawaharlal Nehru, who had certain attributes of modernity that Gandhi lacked. He possessed a capacity to travel in cosmopolitan circles without completely losing touch with the Indian masses. For Nehru, in contrast to Gandhi, steel mills were the new temples to be built, and Fabian socialism was the wave of the future. Nehru was a blend of Brahman aristocrat and British university graduate. It was this combination, incidentally, that inclined him against Americans—a friendly but uncultured lot, as he viewed them. He was a man for whom India alone was not enough. There was a larger world to serve and save. Yet for all his aristocratic demeanor and training, Nehru's intellectual commitments were to democracy, British style. In this respect, he had been well trained.

The Sri Lankan political elite came from a similar mold, even though they traversed a wider political spectrum. Once I had tea and crumpets at the sumptuous home of Sri Lanka's leading Trotskyite; we were served by a maid in formal attire as we discussed local politics, with the visage of Leon Trotsky gazing sternly from the wall. Revolution seemed remote. The mainstream politicians of Sri Lanka were equally urbane, educated, and intense, but they had a sense of what was proper in polite society. As long as such aristocratic democrats could agree on the political rules governing parliamentarism and could tutor their people accordingly, stability was assured, even during transitions in power. Only later, when ethnicity was projected into the center of the Sri Lankan political arena, was the system threatened.

The British governors and teachers had greater problems in shaping elites in Muslim countries. Western secularism coexisted uneasily with the concept of a state built on religious exclusivism, even if the latter stopped short of full-fledged Islamic fundamentalism. Nonetheless, in Pakistan a sizable portion of the elite manifested a commitment in principle to democratic political institutions, together with an economic pragmatism that owed much to yet another strand of British thought and practice. Quite possibly, however, it was in the military men of Pakistan that one saw the strongest evidence of British influence. Taking advantage of the pronounced martial strain in Muslim culture, British instructors honed trainees into a modern military force that was to rule the societies of Pakistan and Bangladesh in the years ahead. There is no better example of the fact that British tutelage could lend itself to different outcomes, depending upon indigenous conditions and perceived external threats.

Burma, lying on the periphery of the British Raj and governed by a stubbornly xenophobic elite, may have received less careful attention, but here too the British stamp was to be found upon many of those who initially rose to power. Indeed, sympathetic Britishers, among them the civil servant J. V. Furnivall, helped initiate a number of these individuals into the mysteries of democracy and Fabian socialism when the latter were students and members of the Thakin Society prior to the outbreak of World War II. Later the Japanese likewise made a contribution, providing military training to selected Burmese nationalists. Thus, the first postwar leaders were a mixture of young soldiers and civilians. When the key figure, General Aung San, was assassinated along with other members of his cabinet, U Nu assumed leadership. Gentle, vague, and often enigmatic, U Nu claimed at various times to be both a Marxist and a Buddhist. When asked how he reconciled these seemingly irreconcilable faiths, his answer was, "Maybe I shall be punished in my next life." Whatever his ideological commitments, U Nu and his associates kept to the democratic path. However, their weak leadership and their inability to manage a multiethnic, multireligious society was to lead to grief for them and for their people.

In Malaysia and Singapore, one can see yet again the fascinating versatility of British guidance, and the capacity of the English to shape their methods of governance to accord with conditions at hand, all the while implanting certain basic political principles. Thus, in Malaysia, they made extensive use of royalty and the rest of the aristocracy both for symbolic purposes and to serve as practicing heads of state, but the system itself rested upon parliamentarism despite the society's ethnic complexity. In Singapore, also, parliamentarism survived early difficulties. After a brief, curious period during which this overwhelmingly Chinese city-state was headed by an Iraqi Jew named David Marshall, the leadership was assumed by a bright young man known as Harry Lee or Lee Kuan Yew, another product of British higher education. Like so many others, Lee became a leftist in England. After wandering a bit politically, he eventually defined himself as a socialist-democrat, though in practice he diverged first from socialism and later in some degree from democracy. Nevertheless, at his zenith, Lee set standards for good government that others could emulate.

In Sukarno, Indonesia had a leader who exemplified the Weberian definition of charisma—a man whose strength derived from the mystical, even the religious. Spell-binding as an orator, possessing a magnetic personality, thoroughly Javanese in his superstitions and his way of manipulating others, and generally shrewd in matters political, Sukarno had almost all the attributes of the great leader despite the fact that he progressively misled his nation. Like most of his contemporaries, Sukarno initially subscribed to parliamentarism and socialism. And also like them, he yearned to play a role beyond Indonesia, at both the regional and the global levels.

Another figure regarded by some as charismatic was Ho Chi Minh. Ho's hallmark was his single-minded dedication throughout five decades to the creation of an independent, socialist nation in the Leninist mold. A poorly educated man, a humble servant of the Comintern for many years, a spartan in lifestyle, and a supporter of collective leadership who was never known to have doubts about the values he held or the course he followed, Ho epitomized one type of challenge to the doctrines of liberal democracy. And his was a challenge difficult to meet, since it fused new elements, both of organizational technique and of emotional appeal, with various traditional methods and themes reflecting the Vietnamese way of life.

The postwar leadership of the Philippines stood apart from most others discussed here in several crucial respects. Filipino leaders came from an older generation, one with experience in institutionalized democracy. They reflected the continuity of Philippine politics, a continuity interrupted only by the war years. Legal politics—including political parties, elections, and the accompanying civil liberties—were a part of their political tradition, and were strongly influenced by Filipino culture. For example, the patron-client relationship dominating this and similar societies ruled the political landscape. With few exceptions, moreover, Filipino leaders came from the privileged, mestizo class, representing the well-educated, affluent segment of their society and incorporating diverse elements—Spanish, American, and Chinese, as well as Malay. They were in, but not of, the general region in which they lived. But like other elites of Southeast Asia, their challenge was to alter their society so that it would mesh with the political values to which they paid homage.

The one society of Southeast Asia not under imperialist rule was Thailand. This fact helps explain the relatively mild character of Thai nationalism as well as the enduring nature of its monarchy, an institution that has played a major role in Thailand's modernization. Insufficient homage has been paid to the monarchy as a vehicle for successful evolutionary change in Asia. In Japan and Thailand, the survival of the monarchy permitted loyalty and a sense of nationhood to coalesce around the royal family, and prevented a cult of personality from forming around others. Without becoming too deeply involved in day-to-day administration or overt political activities, the king or queen could help promote modernization in both its political and economic forms, sometimes taking a personal role in advancing the broad goals established by others, encouraging a consensus.

To be sure, the monarchy could also be used for less laudable policies, as happened in Japan during the 1930s. But where the monarchy disappeared—whether because of ineptitude, extensive political involvement, external pressures, or an inability to represent adequately the new nationalist tides—some substitute had to be found, often an individual who assumed the trappings of monarchy without its traditional restraints. Examples can be seen in such diverse societies as North Korea, China, Vietnam, and Burma.

Although Thailand benefited greatly from a forward-looking monarchy and the absence of foreign rule, these circumstances did not prevent political upheavals both before and after World War II, upheavals in which military and the police played increasingly important roles. As in the Philippines, however, older figures were chosen to rule, since Thai politics maintained a basic continuity at a time when new nations were being formed elsewhere.

BEFORE MAKING ANY generalizations about leadership and its tasks in the former colonies of southern Asia, let us explore briefly the situation in those areas of Northeast Asia that had constituted parts of the Japanese empire. Since Manchuria and Taiwan were incorporated into China in one form or another, no indigenous leadership could emerge in these countries. It should be noted, however, that in the case of Taiwan, nearly half a century of Japanese rule had created a people with a sufficient sense of cultural and economic difference to feel deep resentment over mainland China's control, a resentment exacerbated by the brutal Nationalist suppression of the 1947 uprising. The longing of the Taiwanese to be independent was not to disappear—yet another contribution, for better or worse, of a past era of Japanese power.

Korea was a special case, and made more so by the direct involvement of the United States and the Soviet Union. The wisdom of the Yalta agreement, which provided the conditions for Soviet entry into the Pacific War, will long be debated. The agreement's subsequent effect on Korea, however, was the result of a complex series of events. The end of the war came unexpectedly, as the Russians moved swiftly across Manchuria and approached the Korean peninsula from the north. The nearest Americans were in Okinawa. The division of Korea for occupational purposes was intended to be a purely temporary measure. Had no such agreement been reached, Korea would have been unified—under Soviet control. In retrospect, however, it seems naïve to believe that the two great powers could have agreed on unification when basic political and strategic issues were at stake, and when very different leaders and institutions were being fashioned in North and South.

There is no need here to repeat the enormously complex story of postwar Korea. Suffice it to say that the Soviet occupation of the North resulted in a neater, more coherent system than was developed under American aegis in the South. In the North, pliant leadership was available (others were ruthlessly pushed aside) and an orthodox Stalinist system was implanted with minimal difficulty. That system was by no means inconsistent with the native traditions—Korean and Japanese—and the new-style authoritarianism was made easier because dissenters fled toward the South in large numbers, both in the opening stages of the Russian occupation and during the Korean War.

American efforts, in contrast, were marked by confusion and frustration. To encourage multiple leaders and Western-style democratic institutions in the Korea of 1945 can only be described as audacious—or foolhardy. Perhaps predictably, the extremities of the political spectrum outdistanced the center, which was wobbly and uncertain. The distinction between legal and illegal actions was blurred both by the government and by its opponents, since there were few if any commonly accepted rules in the entirely novel democratic game. The existing economic and social system, moreover, provided scant support to the political ideas imported from the United States. Despite Japan's earlier efforts to integrate the country into its empire, Korea was not Japan, either in culture or in stage of development.

The leadership in the two parts of Korea reflected these circumstances. Korean nationalism in both its Communist and non-Communist manifestations had been widely dispersed throughout the Pacific-Asian region since the 1910 annexation. In the early postwar period, indigenous Communists vied in the North with Soviet-Koreans brought from Russia, with Koreans who had long been allies of the Yanan Chinese, and with the so-called Kapsan faction led by Kim Il-song. The Kapsan group had received shelter and training in Siberia during the war. It was Kim whom the Russians anointed and who rose to power after a failed experiment with united-front tactics under the Christian leader Cho Man-sik. Kim and the small group he led were young, had had limited formal education, were ardently nationalist in a provincial, xenophobic sense, and were prepared to be ruthless. Kim himself was highly intelligent and appears to have had some Christian training as well as a close acquaintance with Chinese culture, since he had been brought up in Manchuria. On balance, however, he and his followers were deeply traditional, Marxist rhetoric notwithstanding. To a greater degree than the leadership of any other part of ex-colonial Asia, they came to power devoid of cosmopolitanism, prone to exclusiveness and isolation.

Syngman Rhee, though to some extent an American product, was not an American favorite. The U.S. authorities would have preferred a man like Kim Kyu-sik, but his ascension to power would have required a degree of intervention that the United States was not prepared to undertake. Kim often seemed indecisive, perhaps because of his moderation. Rhee was unquestionably a remarkable man. Having earned an American Ph.D. and lived in the United States for some three decades, he was nevertheless Korean to the core. Like many revolutionaries, Rhee possessed a combination of single-mindedness and unquenchable optimism that had enabled him to survive decades of failure. Intelligent, cantankerous, extreme in his commitment to Korean nationalism and in his hatred of the Japanese, he epitomized that toughness —and authoritarianism—that rested uneasily with his Wilsonian education.

His followers (like Kim Il-song, he demanded absolute loyalty) included a number of individuals who had accommodated to Japanese rule and who in many cases had a complex love-hate relationship with Japan. Rhee was both idealist and politician. His enemies were legion, but he and his supporters built an effective political organization. Until he was deserted by the police and a portion of the military, he reigned supreme, while the uneasy American government tagged along.

WHAT GENERALIZATIONS CAN one make, based on this survey of the first-generation leadership that emerged after 1945 in ex-colonial Asia? First, the importance of that leadership is underscored by the fact that the newly established political and economic institutions were fragile and susceptible to repeated changes. As I have emphasized, it was not institutions but men that moved people and shaped the broad course of the society. Institutions could often be made to fit the outcome or could simply be disregarded. It is also true, however, that with commitment and effective policies, leaders could strengthen the institutions they had inherited or built. In this respect, one must give credit to such diverse first-generation elites as those of India, Malaysia, and Singapore—and, one must add, North Korea. Even in the Philippines and South Korea, the initial institutions survived in the face of multiple challenges for more than a decade, bequeathing a legacy for the future.

Since the first task was essentially political—namely, to build a nation, often out of disparate ethnic, religious, and regional groups—it is not surprising that those first-generation leaders who survived and rose to the top were individuals who possessed the greatest organizational skills and ability to mobilize their people. Their public appearances were performances, their rhetoric was inspirational, and they were movement-oriented. In sum, they had charisma. There were exceptions, to be sure, but they were rare—and their legacy has been ambiguous.

Two types of polities predominated in the ex-colonies during the early years. In North Korea and North Vietnam, a one-party dictatorship was instituted, only slightly camouflaged by the creation of a few tame parties or groups that supposedly represented special segments of the society but that were totally under Communist control. The Leninist system was never difficult to identify. Among the societies adhering to parliamentarism, the overwhelming majority came to have a dominant party that remained in power, whether independently or as the leader of a coalition. Instances of alternation in power through national elections were rare.

This was a natural development, since in many cases the preindependence movement converted itself into the ruling party, thereby retaining nationalist symbolism, leadership, and organizational strength. To be sure, other parties or independent figures often shared offices or acquired power at the subnational levels. The dominant party system, whatever its defects, assured greater continuity and stability while permitting considerable political openness.

As was to be expected, the leaders of this era seldom had technical or specialized training of any sort. They were generalists, skilled primarily in the art of politics. Understandably, economic matters were beyond their competence and, more important, usually outside the mainstream of their interest. To be sure, virtually every one of them wished to be counted a champion of economic development, and they and their associates uttered millions of words in behalf of this cause. But as I have noted, they had come to power for other reasons, by virtue of other talents. Moreover, in many cases, the condition of their society seemed to dictate different priorities: first unity, then development. Only vaguely did they appreciate the fact that there was an indissoluble link between these two requirements. Sadly, the new leaders rarely sought counsel from the few trained economists, scientists, and technicians available at home or from the much larger pool of expertise abroad.

The new leaders' propensity was to follow certain ideological or cultural predispositions. As we have seen, many proclaimed themselves socialists, including most of those adhering to parliamentarism. This was understandable. Western capitalism was associated with imperialism and with an individualistic culture often equated in the Asian mind with selfishness and antisocial behavior. The disdain with which Asian aristocrats—and intellectuals—traditionally viewed "the merchant class" was powerfully projected into the modern era. Even in Western Europe, moreover, socialism was in vogue. Its day had come, and no one wanted to lag behind. Furthermore, throughout the colonial world, the indigenous entrepreneurial class was weak, had limited capital, lacked managerial and technical skills, and was unwilling to take risks. And in many Southeast Asian settings, the commercial class and such industrialists or entrepreneurs as existed were primarily Chinese or Indian, causing additional problems. Who but the state would or could take the initiative?

One of the effects of the commitment to socialism, irrespective of the degree of success or failure, was the rapid emergence of a larger, more powerful bureaucratic class. Far from breaking with the colonial tradition, the new leaders in this respect fortified it. Except in the Leninist states, to be sure, socialism did not advance very far. It was subject to "corruption" of various types, such as sweetheart arrangements between industrialists and government, resulting in monopolies or oligopolies in the private sector. Abetting this tendency, initial economic policies tended to favor import-substitution and to emphasize self-reliance.

Development policies were overwhelmingly urban, often centered on the capital. Thus, the gap between the center and outlying districts grew. Rural development, either in agriculture or in small and medium industry, languished. Little attention was given to population planning. The surplus population naturally poured into the already overcrowded cities. On balance, economic trends were discouraging and scarcely served to support democratic political institutions where these existed. One trend offered hope. Everywhere there was a greater emphasis on education, from primary schooling to overseas training. Although the brain drain resulting from the latter was high, new economic and technological elites as well as a widening pool of skilled labor were in the offing. This development was pregnant with possibilities for the future growth of the private sector.

The political heights, it should be reiterated, were initially controlled principally by civilians. Some civilians, to be sure, had had intimate ties with the military or had actually served in a military or quasi-military capacity, including strategic planning, during the revolutionary era. But they did not think of themselves as—or act like—members of the military class. It was not until civilian governance had failed, or appeared to have failed, that military regimes came into vogue in Asia, as in many other parts of the so-called Third World.

In terms of foreign policy, ex-colonial Asia was divided into three parts. Quite naturally, North Korea and North Vietnam proclaimed themselves part of the socialist camp, and seemed comfortable in that position until the Sino-Soviet cleavage. For a time after 1959, they gave evidence of being members of an Asian socialist bloc, aligning themselves with China and against Khrushchev's Soviet Union. In a classic sense, China began to reassert its influence, using ideology to reestablish some of its historic reach. The minor Communist powers, however, particularly Hanoi, took care not to antagonize Moscow too greatly. The advent of the Cultural Revolution in China and the intensification of the Vietnam conflict, moreover, brought new complexities to the picture. Keeping an equal distance from the two Communist giants was rarely possible for the little Communists, although North Vietnam, aided by the war, maintained such a position reasonably well in the decade after 1965.

Just as naturally, South Korea and the Philippines—together with South Vietnam, Taiwan, and Thailand—allied themselves with the United States. Pakistan also shifted into this position, though somewhat uneasily, and with its primary concern India, not the USSR. The alliances in Asia were merely part of a much broader drama. In the years marking the onset of the Cold War, the Soviet Union had established a structure of buffer-state alliances that extended outward on both sides of the Eurasian continent, encompassing virtually all of Eastern Europe and Asia, reaching further than czarist influence at its zenith. Soviet territory now included the northern island chain below Saghalien to within a few miles of Hokkaido, and, taking into account the alliances with the Communist states of Asia, gave the USSR a significant strategic position in Northeast Asia. Yet those who announced the advent of bipolarism were premature. The USSR was only a regional power, albeit one exercising substantial authority over the region most crucial to a global balance at this point—namely, the Eurasian continent.

Another fact must not be forgotten. While binding its deep wounds after the most devastating war in its history, Russia thought principally in defensive terms even as it advanced. Stalin was essentially a cautious man, especially when it came to the United States. Nevertheless, he and his associates were determined to eliminate permanently the threat of a two-front war, so real in the 1930s and 1940s. Ironically, after little more than a decade, the possibility of trouble on two fronts again arose. On one side was a rebellious Eastern Europe and a rapidly recovering Western Europe backed by the United States; on the other was an estranged China. And U.S. military power was dominant in the Pacific as well as the Atlantic.

If the Soviet Union disillusioned its Asian allies by behavior considered both parsimonious and overbearing as well as by its reluctance to take risks with Washington, the United States, even in the years when it was the sole global power, suffered from a lack of credibility among certain Asian allies. Fueling this concern was the realization that a dispute over basic U.S. strategic policy in the Pacific-Asian region remained unresolved. Should the United States base its containment of Communism in Asia on the great island chain off the Asian mainland, stretching from Japan in the north to the Philippines in the South, and count on the forward deployment of its substantial air and naval forces? Or should it accept responsibility for selected regions on the Asian continent, as it was doing in Europe?

The indecision with respect to Korea and Vietnam and the caution characterizing strategic commitments elsewhere on mainland Asia testify to the uncertainty surrounding U.S. strategic policies. Those favoring an island *cordon sanitaire* strategy argued that American air and sea power alone would not suffice and that American manpower should never be pitted against the countless millions available to a potential Asian foe (China). Whatever the outcome of a conflict, the results would not be commensurate with the costs, they insisted, and in terms of the regional and global balance, a *cordon sanitaire* would suffice to protect the island perimeters. Adherents of the alternative strategy (and both sides contained a mix of military and civilian proponents) asserted that the security of islands like Japan was inextricably linked with the need for some continental buffer. A solidly Communist mainland Asia, they insisted, would render the island enclaves vulnerable in every respect. Moreover, morale would sink everywhere if the United States abandoned its Asian allies when they were threatened. Such a policy, in addition to being immoral, would encourage further Communist aggression. Had the lesson of Munich been forgotten?

As the policy pendulum swung first in one direction, then in the other, the United States confused both its friends and its foes. Yet at what proved to be a heavy cost, U.S. military support was extended to continental allies until the deepening of the Sino-Soviet cleavage and other developments such as those in Indonesia changed the strategic map of the Pacific-Asian region.

Meanwhile, apart from the postwar Asian allies of the USSR and the United States a larger number of ex-colonial Asian states proclaimed themselves "neutral," a term predating "nonaligned." In this period, neutralism could have its maximum validity, since the global and regional economic-political-security configurations that were later to emerge had not yet made their debut. Economies, subsequently to be the prime source of interdependence, were more self-contained, and the appeal of independence took precedence over other considerations. Nevertheless, a portion of the idealism marking this strongly ideological age was directed toward the attempt to forge stronger links among Asians—a new type of Pan-Asianism—that would overcome the colonial legacy according to which neighboring societies were strangers and had close ties only with their colonial governing power. It was also hoped that by achieving a greater unity while standing aloof from either of the major power blocs, a Third Force could make itself heard at the global level.

The first monument to this effort was the Bandung Conference of 1955, preceded by the drafting of the Five Principles of Peaceful Coexistence. But the Bandung meeting was not merely a conclave of "neutrals." It also represented an initial attempt to bridge ideological differences among emerging Asian states, with China's Zhou Enlai playing a prominent role along with Nehru, Sukarno, and U Nu. However, the hope that historic rivalries and the problems bequeathed by the colonial era could be quickly or easily overcome was to prove illusory, particularly since the developmental process and its attendant economic needs had not yet proceeded sufficiently far to provide powerful materialistic incentives for cooperation. Various conflicts between Asians followed the Korean War, prominent among them the India-Pakistan, Sino-Indian, and Indonesian-Malaysian struggles. The split between Malaysia and Singapore and the seemingly endless ethnic tensions that rent Burma (among other countries) testified to the fact that security was at least as much a domestic problem as one of foreign relations. In the course of these various struggles, leaders were tarnished, idealism faded, and political openness—where it existed—was threatened. Quite naturally, the military assumed greater importance virtually everywhere in Asia, even in states where they did not seize power. In sum, events proved that neither neutralism nor alliance was a guaranteed route to security.

One final consideration warrants attention. Understandably, the first-generation ex-colonial societies held complex attitudes toward the states that had ruled them. Generally, their feelings toward the British and Americans were warm, although they expected a great deal in the way of aid, and when less was delivered, resentment could flare up. The Dutch and French, having fought colonial wars, were less appreciated, but a strong cultural legacy remained, which especially affected the colonial elites. Korean animosity toward Japan, and vice versa, seemed to explode in the early postwar years, partly because it had deep roots and partly because it was politically cultivated. In general, however, a combination of cultural, economic, and security factors served to support old ties—sometimes after a decent interval. With second- and third-generation leaders, however, the bonds loosened, often promoting different attitudes.

LET ME NOW turn to leadership and policy in noncolonial Asia, focusing on China and Japan during the early postwar era. As I have already suggested, the challenges confronting the Kuomintang as a result of the Sino-Japanese conflict were enormous, and they remained unmet. The mistakes made by the Nationalists after the Japanese surrender encompassed economic, political, and strategic matters. Currency policies in combination with the economic mismanagement of "liberated China" virtually wiped out the middle class, and inflation reached astronomical proportions. Little effort was made to cultivate China's Third Force, those politically active individuals who had chosen to affiliate with neither the Nationalists nor the Communists. Indeed, the intellectuals who constituted a significant portion of this force were deeply alienated by the increasingly heavy-handed treatment meted out to them by Nationalist military and police authorities. Morale within Nationalist ranks, moreover, was at low ebb, and corruption was rampant.

Naturally, the Communists both incited events and took advantage of them. Ceaselessly they organized, propagandized, and conducted a wide range of underground activities in the Nationalist heartland. In a time of near chaos, there was a signal advantage in being out of power, hence able to play the role of trenchant critic and attracting a growing number of dissidents to one's side.

On the military front, the Nationalists first blundered by not absorbing the "puppet troops" of the Wang Jingwei government. The Communists had no hesitation about using "enemy troops," reindoctrinating them to the extent possible. It was also a major mistake to attempt to wrest Manchuria away from the Communists when the lines of communications and supply could not be maintained. Some of the best Nationalist troops surrendered when they were surrounded and cut off from reinforcements, setting the stage for the military disasters that were to follow. Finally, it was later revealed that the Communists had managed to subvert one of the highest Nationalist intelligence officers, giving them access to Kuomintang military plans.

Nationalist leaders later blamed the United States for putting heavy pressure on them to negotiate with the Communists at a time when they might have been able to deal the Communists a decisive military blow. In retrospect, the Marshall Mission was probably destined to fail. The united fronts being constructed between non-Communists and Communists in Western Europe at this point could not provide a model for China. Neither the Chinese Communists nor the Nationalists had had experience with Western-style parliamentarism, nor was either party in a mood to share power. A complete lack of trust, based on experience, existed on both sides. Most important, the coalitions created in Western Europe did not have to overcome the existence of separate armies and, in effect, separate states, as was currently the case in China. Thus, it can be argued that the mission headed by General George Marshall was a mistake, since it was doomed to failure. Unquestionably it delayed the renewal of large-scale civil war by some months. But the collapse of Kuomintang China resulted essentially from domestic factors, some long en route, others of recent vintage. American policies were a peripheral element.

The first-generation Chinese Communist leaders were a mixture of petty intellectuals and soldiers of peasant background. By using the phrase "petty intellectuals," I do not mean to denigrate the intelligence of men like Mao Zedong, Zhou Enlai, and Deng Xiaoping. Clearly they were very intelligent. Rather, I mean that in comparison to the official intellectual class of China, their educational background had been meager and their way of life shaped by long years of rural warfare. Despite a few sophisticates like Zhou, most first-generation Communist leaders, including Mao, were "country people" as opposed to urbanites, and many had an instinctive distrust of cities and city dwellers, notwithstanding certain policies subsequently pursued. Mao himself had a lifelong love-hate relationship with intellectuals, reflecting in part his resentment of his treatment at Peking University as a lowly library assistant. He was never enrolled as a student there or at any other university. And until 1949 he had never been beyond eastern China. Having no concern for wealth or appearance, Mao devoted his attention to politics with one objective: power. Proud, suspicious, incapable of forming a lasting relationship of trust with any individual, man or woman, he died as he had lived—a lonely, frustrated person. Above all, Mao was quintessentially Chinese. Despite his efforts, he could not encompass, emotionally or even intellectually, the cosmopolitanism that constituted such an important part of Marxism.

It scarcely needs to be said that Mao made an enormous difference to China in the years that followed Communist victory. Yet in the early stages of Communist rule, the program of the Chinese Communist Party, both political and economic, was closely modeled after that of Stalinist Russia, despite some important distinctions. Leninism called for tutelage similar to but vastly more intensive than that which China had previously known. It also demanded a high degree of centralization despite the country's great size and heterogeneity, and a party-state system that aimed at making politics dominant over every aspect of the society. Although this did not—could not—succeed, more Chinese were drawn into the political process than any time in that nation's history. At both the apex and at the ward or village level, the party guided, guarded, and exhorted, but what was most different was the relatively tight linkage down the chain of command, and the competition that the party now offered with private governance, including that of the family.

Behind the party, or, more accurately, interwoven with it, were the police and the military. In the opening phases of the Communist era, indeed, military men were at the helm in the major regions into which China had been divided. Law and order were imposed on an unprecedented scale after the initial turmoil of rural class warfare, which caused the deaths of millions and fundamentally altered China's rural class structure. But as in the USSR, China's military leaders were indoctrinated to think of themselves as party members first, subject to party policies and orders. The hierarchical chain of party-military command extended throughout an ever greater part of the nation. The warlordism of the past faded, although military privilege and power remained very much a part of the scene. In the first years of the new order, moreover, a process of role differentiation was initiated, not totally dissimilar to that of early Meiji Japan, whereby military men assumed purely administrative functions in government, even in technical fields. Only when the party was virtually destroyed in the course of the Cultural Revolution did those who had command of the guns once again assume direct political authority.

Whereas Leninism prevailed in the political realm, Stalinism was the model in the economic sphere. The land reform program moved rapidly from redistribution on a private basis to cooperatives, and then to collectivization. More closely mirroring the Soviet model was the big push toward heavy industry. Thousands of Soviet experts and billions of Soviet rubles were devoted to this program. Blessed with peace, provided (at least initially) with incentives, and aided by new technology, the Chinese peasant and worker broke productivity records. Confidence among leaders, including Mao, soared.

Yet even in this period, the Soviet model demonstrated its flaws when applied to China. How could urban industrialization be favored over rural development when the peasants were so numerous and so poor? The commune system and the Great Leap Forward were ill-considered attempts to solve this problem. Fundamental differences over developmental issues were a factor in the Sino-Soviet cleavage, but they played a much more important part in splitting the Chinese Communist elite after 1958.

By the 1960s, Mao and Maoism had brought deep trouble, both politically and economically, to China. It is possible that as many as twenty million Chinese died between 1959 and 1961, from a combination of harsh weather and totally misguided government policies which caused widespread food shortages. Mao had to step back after this catastrophe, allowing Liu Shaoqi and Deng Xiaoping to undertake more rational policies. But intrigue in the succeeding years was ceaseless as men vied over policy and power, leading up to the so-called Cultural Revolution. No person or group had the combination of courage and authority to enforce a change of top leadership and basic policy. In line with the proclivities of the Stalinist system, Mao's colleagues had elevated him to an unassailable position from which he could topple all of them. The world was thus treated to the extraordinary spectacle of personalized and increasingly irrational rule at the apex of a giant bureaucratic pyramid—Leninism in its pure Stalinist form, but also in line with China's own political history. The saga of an aging emperor, enfeebled by a stroke and assorted other ills, insulated from the world by a small coterie of retainers, was not new to this ancient land. Indeed, Chinese politics in Mao's final years represented a curious amalgam of medievalism and modernity, reflecting the idiosyncrasies of both a man and a society forced to live in many different epochs simultaneously.

China's foreign policy in the opening years of Communist rule testified to the influence of three forces: nationalism, or, more accurately, the leaders' perception of national interest; ideology, now Marxism-Leninism, as interpreted and applied by Beijing; and tradition, namely the continuation of certain historic attitudes and modes of behavior. The first two elements combined to underwrite the alliance with the USSR. A common enemy and a common ideology, supplemented by China's developmental needs, served to bring China and Russia together. Considering the grievous damage it had suffered during the war, Soviet assistance to China was generous and enormously important to the initial economic spurt. More important, however, the massive Russian military presence on the Eurasian continent provided security against the perceived American threat.

Why did the Sino-Soviet alliance—an alliance of potentially awesome consequences for Eurasia and the world—disintegrate in less than a decade? From the beginning, there were differences over various matters connected with Soviet aid, and later the Chinese were to find fault with Russian technology. These were not the issues that precipitated the break, however. It would also be a mistake to believe that either side had grave reservations about their new relationship, or that a friendlier United States at this point would have produced a "neutral" Communist China. The latter myth has been woven into later arguments over the China policy of the United States, but however one judges those policies, it is naïve to assume that if the United States had switched sides or reached out to the Communists (actions difficult to contemplate in any case under the prevailing circumstances), Mao and his associates could have been separated from the socialist camp in the 1940s. Despite their staunch nationalist commitments—and their strong identification with Chinese culture—the overwhelming majority of Chinese Communist leaders, including Mao, considered themselves good Marxist-Leninists and members of an international socialist camp headed by the Great Soviet Union. Lenin was to be revered, Stalin to be honored. It took many events, spread over some years, to shake Chinese Communist faith in the Soviet Union. The seeds of distrust were present, to be sure, but they had to be nurtured by actual experiences.

For their part, the Russian leaders, putting aside for the time being their historic fear of the Yellow Peril, saw in the tie with China a means to guarantee the security of the Soviet Far East. With China, moreover, it was possible to think of a new global strength, and one that could be of significance in relations with the rest of the developing world. Thus, at this point, the Sino-Soviet alliance was eminently logical from the standpoint of both parties, and the fact that basic geopolitical considerations weighed against its permanence should not blind one to the realities of the 1940s.

In the early years of the People's Republic, while it paraded its internationalist banners before the world, an acute sense of national interests—and the limitations imposed by the conditions prevailing in China—were always kept in mind. Revolutionary rhetoric was dispensed in abundance. The costs and risks involved in such activities were slight. Moreover, modest assistance was given revolutionary movements elsewhere. But of military power, China had little, and when it was employed against the United States, the cost was high, as illustrated by the Korean War. In part, ideology served as a substitute for power, giving the Chinese a sense of belonging to a global movement that had momentum on its side. Like the early Bolsheviks, the Chinese revolutionaries of this period believed, or said they believed, that the revolutionary surge in the non-Western world would sweep all before it. And there was another consideration. As Zhou Enlai remarked, if China could release ten fleas, the United States, in attempting to catch them with its ten fingers, would lose them all. By supplying even modest support to revolutionary movements, a weak and impoverished China could effectively strike back at the United States.

Chinese nationalism, however, cut diverse ways, especially when colored by traditional attitudes. China's leaders were not prepared to abandon their "Middle Kingdom" views merely because they had espoused Marxism-Leninism. One still had to deal with barbarians on the frontiers, and had to reward or punish them as their actions merited. Neighboring small countries were never allowed to forget that China was, or would become, a great power.

Nationalism also played a prominent part in the breakup of the Sino-Soviet alliance—a fascinating and vitally significant development. The seeds of distrust and resentment began to sprout after the death of Stalin. Personal factors were not absent. Mao had looked upon Stalin as his teacher, but he saw no reason to accord Khrushchev homage. The new Russian leader was junior both in age and in experience. Moreover, his style was soon judged crude and unpredictable. After a brief honeymoon period, a rift opened between Khrushchev and the Chinese, and further widened when the Soviet leader attacked Stalin in 1956 without giving the Chinese or other foreign Communists advance notice. Having praised Stalin unstintingly before their own people and throughout the world, Mao and his associates felt humiliated. In truth, Khrushchev was forced by events to put the struggle to reorient Soviet domestic politics and policies ahead of international Communist solidarity. This fact, long minimized, should be emphasized.

The anti-Stalin campaign was, to the Chinese, but one of many signs of Russian overlordship. First privately, then publicly, the Chinese leaders called for equality within Communist ranks and for the recognition of the sovereignty of each Communist state. Their criticisms of "those who wave their baton and expect others to follow" grew progressively sharper. Meanwhile, Mao's commune experiment was drawing Russian criticism—amply justified, as events proved. But the fundamental cause of the split came when Khrushchev seemed to indicate that détente with the United States (enabling him to pursue domestic reforms) was more important than Soviet military risks on behalf of China. As tensions mounted, the Russians also thought better of having offered the Chinese assistance in developing their nuclear program. With these events as a context for the second Taiwan Straits crisis and its aftermath in 1958–1959, the principal raison d'être of the alliance disappeared, as far as the Chinese were concerned. If the Soviets were not credible as an ally, what purpose did the alliance serve?

By 1960, although still largely hidden from the world, the quarrel had moved into an ugly stage. The Russians withdrew their technicians, even the blueprints for unfinished projects, adding to the crisis that had been brought on by the Great Leap Forward. At this point, moreover, ideological confrontations heaped additional fuel on the fire. Each side sought to read the other out of the Leninist church, and in doing so to challenge the other side's legitimacy before the global Communist congregation. Acrimonious disputes took place at various international conferences and Communist Party meetings.

For China, the 1960s were bitter years. The country paid a heavy price for the serious errors in domestic economic policies, and as one result, deep fissures opened up within top Communist ranks. Mistakes in Chinese foreign policy paralleled those on the domestic front. With the Sino-Soviet alliance smashed beyond repair, the Chinese proclaimed themselves aligned with the Third World against the First World (the United States and the USSR) and aloof from the Second World (the capitalist countries of Europe and Japan). However reflective of China's status this policy was, and however comforting ideologically, it could not satisfy either of the two critical desiderata of any Chinese foreign policy: security and development. Thus, when the Soviet military threat loomed up at the end of the 1960s, China did not have the strength to either negotiate or fight with the Russians. A new policy was imperative.

WHAT AN EXTRAORDINARY contrast existed between developments in China and those taking place in Japan during these same years. In considering the reconstruction of the Japanese state after 1945, two equally important factors warrant consideration. First, there was much in prewar Japan upon which to build, in political as well as economic terms. Competitive politics and parliamentarism were not novelties to the Japanese, despite the flawed legacy of prewar democracy. And more than any other Asian state, Japan was at a socioeconomic stage appropriate for democratic experimentation. Second, certain basic changes were essential if a new Japan was to be born, and these could best be made quickly by an external force. To put it differently, the stage of Japanese development and the proclivities of the United States meshed exceedingly well.

In the brief period of punishment and reform, several political developments occurred in Japan which were to have long-range implications. The revisions in political institutions removed the two threats to democracy so prominent in the prewar era: imperial sovereignty and the dual structure that gave the military independent power. In addition, a new segment of the old elite was elevated to leadership through a combination of U.S. and Japanese actions. The Americans forcibly removed those members of the old elite who were viewed as responsible for the war, including the entire military hierarchy. The Japanese, after some indecision, proceeded by means of elections to install individuals from the liberal wing of the conservative movement in power, among them leaders of the Anglo-American branch of the foreign ministry.

From this beginning, Japan evolved a dominant party system while retaining the essential requirements of a democracy. Many interrelated factors were involved: the creation and maintenance of a formidable coalition among business, the urban middle class, and agriculture; the ruling party's access to ample funds; recognized, experienced leadership; an electoral system favoring the conservatives; and divisions and weaknesses within the opposition. But two additional elements were vitally important: first, the policies promoted by the conservatives (who became the Liberal Democratic Party in 1955) were eminently successful, and, second, given the factional make-up of Japanese politics, one could change leaders without changing parties.

Some insisted that since the bureaucratic component in Japanese policy making was high, since top leadership was determined from within the party, not by the electorate, and since power did not alternate via elections, Japan did not deserve to be considered a full-fledged democracy. In my view, this argument is specious. Democracy requires only that the citizenry be given the widest choice in selecting its representatives, and hence its government, from among various alternatives. Second, the fullest range of political freedoms must exist to ensure the citizenry access to information in making that choice. Within these perimeters, a variety of democratic systems is possible, and is to be found in our times.

If the Japanese postwar political system was unique, it was by virtue of its leadership. Certain leaders stood out, especially to the external world. Yoshida Shigeru and, more recently, Nakasone Yasuhiro are examples. Yet those corporate qualities of Japan that I emphasized earlier tended to subordinate the individual leader to a collective decision-making process and place a premium upon his role as coordinator and conciliator rather than innovator. The inner, private roles exceeded the external, public roles in importance.

Meanwhile, in fostering economic development, Japanese leaders once again built upon the past. By the end of World War II, Japan had had three-quarters of a century's experience in constructing a modern economic system, and in the previous decade, industrial development had spurted ahead at an accelerating rate. Given proper domestic policies and compatible international conditions, Japan was ready for an economic take-off. The secret of Japan's success was no secret. The Japanese miracle was no miracle. With initial American assistance and the subsequent encouragement, guidance, and orders of the Japanese government, policies were advanced that maximized Japan's accrued advantages and took account of the existing international environment. At the broadest level, both socialism and laissez-faire policies were rejected in favor of a partnership between the state and the private sector, a partnership that worked to the benefit of both. Blessed with political stability and social harmony, Japan achieved a consensus on adopting an export-oriented strategy at a time when the Japanese industrial sector was ready, the American market was available, the world—and especially the advanced world—was generally prosperous and at peace, the price ratio between raw materials (including energy) and manufactured products was highly favorable for industrial products, and it was possible to acquire—by one means or another—advanced technology quickly. The major innovations for which Japan should be credited are these: achieving a constructive symbiosis between state planning and private initiatives; maintaining protectionism without unduly restricting domestic competition; and preserving a social system with gradual modifications in the midst of extraordinarily rapid economic growth, thereby underwriting stability.

As one reflects upon the American Occupation and its contributions to Japan's subsequent development, it is possible to miss America's most significant gift. That gift was not democratic institutions, although these were important. It was not economic assistance in its various forms, although that proved to be very valuable, since it came at a critical time. The greatest gift was to remove from Japan the costs and risks of a high-profile foreign policy. Japan was given the freedom to pursue a market foreign policy, with the United States providing the major market, assuming the security burdens, and defending Japanese interests in the face of a somewhat hostile world.

It is thus not surprising that Japanese foreign policy in these years was firmly tied to the United States. Here was an alliance typical of those of the early post-1945 period. The major power—in this case, the United States—gave virtually unconditional assurances of security and economic assistance in case of need; and the lesser party—in this case, Japan—provided firm pledges of political allegiance. Such an alliance was not one of equals or partners. That was impossible under the circumstances. But there were advantages to both sides. And in this particular case, it was so obviously advantageous to Japan that despite a challenge mounted against the alliance in 1960, even the opposition parties (with the exception of the Communists) gradually ceased to attack it directly.

LET ME NOW integrate the principal themes I set forth earlier. From the vantage point of the 1960s, the broad trends in Asia were not reassuring. It could be argued, of course, that the time that had elapsed since the war had ended and many new states had been created was far too short to permit young political institutions to take firm hold or economic programs to show results. This was true, but concern over certain adverse and possibly irreversible trends seemed warranted. With the defeat of Japan and the retreat of the West, a buoyant optimism had prevailed among the young leaders taking power in the early postwar years. Yet the tasks of achieving national unification and launching successful developmental programs had proven vastly more difficult than anticipated. Almost everywhere, parliamentarism was in retreat or under siege. Civilian governance was giving way to military rule, and this in itself was a sign of failure and dissatisfaction. It seemed doubtful whether societies could bridge the deep chasm between liberal political institutions and a socioeconomic structure that was still largely traditional. The easier route was via authoritarianism. But could authoritarian governments devise a better economic strategy? Granting the need for planning and a significant role for the state, most current policies seemed aimless, fostering bureaucratism, inefficiency, debt, and corruption—stunting rather than stimulating growth, and keeping productivity at a low level.

There were exceptions, of course, prominent among them Japan. And for the first time, a few other leaders such as those in South Korea saw in the Japanese model a potential that was absent from the Western and Soviet systems. Moreover, democratic institutions were surviving even in some states where social and economic problems appeared formidable; and in the very act of surviving, they were acquiring legitimacy, or, at a minimum, were cultivating habits of political behavior. Few if any of the first-generation leaders, it might be noted, abandoned their initial political convictions, however sorely tested. Nonetheless, the most basic trends were disquieting.

The Leninist states of Asia were certainly not in better condition. China, where at the beginning the promises of a new unity and vigorous economic growth under socialism had seemed to shine so brightly, was headed toward progressively deeper political turmoil in the 1960s. The economy was also in serious trouble. The Cultural Revolution remains one of the truly bizarre events of the twentieth century. Is it to be explained as a manifestation of Mao's growing antipathy to the bureaucratism, elitist privilege, and abandonment of principle (as he viewed it) of the Communist Party and state, and as the renewed expression of that part of the man that was individualist, iconoclastic, even anarchist? If so, the paradox was mind-boggling, since it was Mao who had helped to create and lead the most bureaucratic, authoritarian, hierarchical political system that China had ever known. Or is the Cultural Revolution to be explained on a more elemental level—namely, as the actions of a man increasingly resentful of having been relegated to a back row after the failures of earlier experiments, progressively isolated from reality and paranoid about enemies, real and imagined? Or was an aging man misled and manipulated by a coterie of self-serving individuals, including his wife, most of them previously far from the center of power and eager to topple "the usurpers of the throne"? Perhaps the truth lies in some combination of these explanations. In any case, the supreme leader suddenly moved to bring down the party and state he had created, shrewdly mobilizing those external forces with which he had been historically associated: China's students and soldiers. In the middle stages of the upheaval that ensued, domestic events and foreign policies were so irrational that some observers spoke of China as suffering from a nervous breakdown. Only the fact that the Chinese had a high threshold of tolerance for chaos preserved the society. But at its zenith, the Cultural Revolution imposed Mao's isolation on an entire nation. China was bereft of all friends—except Albania.

North Korea (the Democratic People's Republic of Korea, or DPRK), where the political system was as close to totalitarianism as a humanly operated society could come, had a relatively good economic record. In the Japanese era, the North had contained the bulk of Korea's mining and industry, whereas the South had been heavily agricultural. Then came the carnage of the Korean War. Utilizing Soviet bloc assistance, modern plants arose amid the ashes of the old factories. Meanwhile, the government encouraged scientific agriculture, with impressive initial results. By the late 1960s, however, Pyongyang was troubled by heavy military expenditures, combined with the growing problems resulting from being largely shut off from the latest technology.

There was something at once primitive and awesome about this society. Class distinctions were rigorously maintained, and for those who came from "bourgeois" or gentry families, the future was bleak. Yet the new privileged classes of a Communist state so brilliantly depicted by Djilas were easily identifiable in North Korea: the higher party cadres and military officers. And none was more privileged than Kim Il-song and his family. Kim had eliminated his principal rivals by the end of the Korean War, and after 1956 his control was never seriously challenged. Around him and his family arose a cult of personality rarely if ever equaled. And the DPRK was eulogized before its people in myriad ways as a paradise on earth. Did the citizenry believe? The evidence suggests that the combination of lifelong indoctrination and isolation was very effective. Perhaps the negative themes were as powerful in inducing unity as the positive ones. Every North Korean was taught that to confront the power of American imperialism and the numerical superiority of the "South Korean puppets," he must exhibit the strength of ten and must never waver from the iron-clad solidarity provided by the party. Among the few defectors, an overwhelming majority came from "bad class backgrounds" or had other personal reasons for their deviation. Yet how long could the medieval citadel stand in a world undergoing truly revolutionary changes?

North Vietnam, one of Asia's poorer countries, was mobilized to fight a combined civil-international war. Feeling themselves betrayed by their Soviet and Chinese allies at the 1954 Geneva Conference, the Vietnam Communist leaders had no desire for international supervisors to enter their precincts or for verified national elections, although the Diem government in Saigon saved them from having to articulate that position. When the South failed to collapse as it was supposed to do and the Saigon government began to decimate the Communist underground, the decision was made to "liberate" the Republic of Vietnam by force. What would have been Hanoi's decision at the time had its leaders known that within a few years, approximately half a million American soldiers would be in Vietnam? As in the case of Korea, the United States sent out confusing, contradictory signals. But by the mid-1960s, large-scale conflict was underway, and for North Vietnam, development could be no more than a distant dream; the first task was to defeat the enemy using all available means, political as well as military, and to direct these at the South Vietnamese, the Americans, and the world. For Hanoi, but not for Washington, this was total war.

The smallest Communist state in Asia, the People's Republic of Mongolia, rested in the Soviet shadow in its customary somnolence. In the early 1920s, certain Mongols had turned to the Bolsheviks to protect them against China. Through the years, the Russians had remained their only credible source of security, and though the price was a high degree of Sovietization, there seemed to be but one alternative: a return to subsidiary status as a backward part of the Chinese empire.

If domestic conditions in much of Asia—both Communist and non-Communist—were depressing, regional relations were scarcely more promising as the 1960s drew to a close. Relations among the Pacific-Asian states were only occasionally constructive and cordial, especially when ideological lines had to be crossed or when divided states were involved. China seemed prepared to antagonize almost everyone, and Sino-Soviet relations, then at low ebb, threatened to break into open conflict. The hostility between North and South Korea appeared implacable. Taiwan represented an unresolved issue that at times seemed likely to lead to further bloodshed.

In Southeast Asia, the situation was equally ominous. The struggle throughout Indochina was gradually involving all of the major nations, as well as smaller states like Thailand, South Korea, and the Philippines. Indonesia suddenly loomed as a separate threat to its neighbors.

The Indian subcontinent was also involved in hot and cold wars, especially between India and Pakistan, but also between India and China. The spirit of Bandung—the euphonious talk about peaceful coexistence—had largely disappeared. And like a great shadow over the entire region, the American-Soviet confrontation continued. Some of the problems troubling Asian international relations had their origin in the distant past; they had been interrupted by the colonial era but were now reemerging. Others were new, the products of aggressive nationalism, ideological confrontation, or even the need to distract the people from domestic crises.

Asia, it should be noted, was not necessarily in worse shape than other parts of the so-called Third World. In fact, it could be argued that in reality, and particularly in terms of potential, its picture was brighter. Yet viewed from the perspective of the late 1960s, pessimism seemed warranted. Except in a few countries, neither political stability nor coherent developmental policies had been achieved. Externally, hostility or aloofness among Pacific-Asian states was the dominant feature, albeit with security ties to the two major powers providing protection for certain states. Why and how did this relatively dismal picture change in the two decades that followed?

3 | *Evolution and Revolution: Variations on Change*

AS THE TWENTIETH CENTURY draws toward a close, we see that three basic political systems have taken root in Asia. The Leninist system, the most easily identifiable, represents an effort to capitalize on the ideological and organizational frontiers of modern politics while retaining the elitist controls and constraints associated with traditional systems.

The authoritarian-pluralist system, more widely dispersed then Leninism, is a compromise intended to fit the nature and perceived needs of a society at a given stage of development. It gives priority to political unity but accepts or even encourages economic and social pluralism—the acknowledged sources of growth.

The liberal democratic system, a relative rarity, is based on the gamble that the political accountability derived from competition will produce benefits outweighing the costs of disunity, and that political pluralism is essential to social and economic dynamism.

In terms of performance, how does one evaluate these three systems at this time, granting they vary in numerous and important ways from country to country? And what trends can one discern both within and across these systems?

LET ME TURN first to contemporary Leninism in Asia. Despite the significant differences among Asian Leninist societies, it is possible to advance certain generalizations. First, the Stalinist "big push" economic model, with its emphasis on heavy industry, strongly centralized controls, and agrarian collectivization, is under assault. At the same time, an effort to encourage political inclusiveness in new forms is underway in certain Leninist states. The channels of information and communication both within the society and to the external world are being widened. The citizen is being given somewhat greater opportunity to participate meaningfully in political processes, including the selection of leaders and the determination of policies. The old mass indoctrination and mobilization tactics that were intended to underwrite party and state legitimacy while also providing pliant subjects are being altered in an effort to generate genuine rather than mechanistic participation.

One should not exaggerate what has happened thus far. It is too early to be certain that current trends will be sustained and expanded; but given their context, it seems increasingly probable that we are witnessing the most profound changes in Leninist societies since the Bolshevik Revolution—changes that may warrant our speaking of a second revolution auguring the irreversible demise of Leninism.

There is much about this revolution that defies classical theories, especially Marxism. It comes not because Leninist societies have reached a new developmental stage, but because stagnation threatens. This decline, moreover, has been appreciated most fully by certain members of the political elite, those charged with matching the performance of the so-called capitalist or advanced industrial nations. It is they, not the masses, who are in the vanguard in seeking to promote new values and policies, frequently in the name of patriotism, of building a strong and wealthy country able to compete with others in the twenty-first century. There is a remarkable similarity between this theme and that which motivated the Meiji leaders of Japan a century ago.

Why is this revolution motivated by and led from the top? The answer is simply that it could have come from nowhere else. Leninism did not equip the ordinary citizen to lead a dynamic movement dedicated to fundamental change. Herein lie some of the most serious problems in establishing a new order. Expanded literacy and a greater flow of information are not sufficient, if ritualized participation in politics has been the only norm and if political institutions are subordinated to personalized rule. A new emperor or czar, however enlightened, does not represent a structural change. Nor are science and technology sufficient, if an entrepreneurial spirit and the incentives for creative labor are absent. It is in these respects that a genuine revolution is required. The "new socialist man" heralded in Communist literature is not equipped, either in economic or political terms, to lead his society into a new age. Thus, a basic cultural transformation is necessary, a new mix of attitudes and behavior that can alter the stultifying culture shaped by the Leninist system. Only insofar as new policies lead to this end will the revolution now underway succeed.

China, like the Soviet Union, testifies to this fact. It should be acknowledged that the Stalinist strategy pursued in the opening years of Chinese Communist rule had certain benefits. Public health improved, for example, and life expectancy increased—a mixed blessing, to be sure. Mass education at the primary level was extended, making literacy more widespread. An extensive mobilization of manpower and resources for the attainment of selected goals caused production to expand rapidly and created an impressive industrial base for the society. Investment rates remained high and consumption was strictly controlled. Yet the costs of this economic strategy steadily rose. Quantity took priority over quality. Waste and inefficiency were rife. The work ethic declined as people came to realize that the iron rice bowl could not be broken. These and other problems testified to the utter irresponsibility that Stalinist economics engendered at every level of society. And never were the results more dismal than when incentives were taken away from the peasant.

The impetus for reform in China grew out of the political and economic events of two decades, beginning in 1958. Excesses led to failures, and failures produced divisions in the top elite. These in turn resulted in a fierce struggle for power that humiliated but did not liquidate a large proportion of the first-generation Communist leaders, thereby providing an elite receptive to change. Stalin killed his supposed opponents. Mao allowed his perceived rivals to live, sentencing them to internal exile. Thus, in China, the opposition was able to mount a broad-based political attack within a relatively short time. Deng Xiaoping and his associates turned the Cultural Revolution to their advantage, citing it as China's great negative lesson.

The first major monument to the economic reforms, as is well known, was the family responsibility system in agriculture, whereby the farmer was given incentives to increase production. Agricultural reform has certainly not eliminated all problems in China's vast rural areas. Indeed, it has produced new ones: a disinclination to grow grain in favor of selected commercial crops for the sake of earning higher profits, despite the extremely large grain subsidies provided by the state; rising income disparities both among and within regions; excessive consumption and reduced savings rates in rural areas; and the urgent need for larger public investment to support a better infrastructure, including roads, water conservancy, and a host of other necessities. Nevertheless, the return of land to individual families together with the explosive growth of rural industry has resulted in higher living standards and a new dynamism among a sizable number of people—nearly 80 percent of those Chinese who are accounted rural. This fact ensures that whatever else may happen, no government in Beijing is likely to attempt to reimpose rural collectivization.

Not surprisingly, urban reforms have been far more difficult. All of the old sins and deficiencies now exact their costs. Decentralization and managerial control in industry are essential, but they raise complex issues, political as well as economic in nature. The socialist years have produced factory heads that are state managers but not entrepreneurs, and workers that have neither the skills nor the incentive to be efficient. If decentralization merely transfers power from Beijing to the provincial and local governments, the bureaucracy may become even more dominant and entrepreneurship may be even further retarded, as has often proved to be the case. Furthermore, there is some question as to whether managers can really wrest plant authority away from party cadres despite new regulations; their respective abilities will be a key variable. In the absence of unemployment compensation and other adequate social security measures, moreover, how far can they go in insisting upon a rationalized, efficient workforce?

Inseparably connected with these issues is the vexatious question of price reform. If prices bear no relation to the costs of production, if massive subsidies protect ailing factories or industries (as well as eat up the national budget), plant efficiency can never be realized. Yet if a process of deregulation gets underway when production costs remain high and production is limited, inflation is certain, as is now the case. This is a greater problem because China is afflicted with overconsumption in terms of per capita income, a product of the citizens' awareness of the treasures available in today's world. And when a taxi driver makes more than a college professor and a suburban farmer more than an urban doctor, it is not surprising that those seeking higher education—individuals who will be needed in every field to promote China's modernization—are deeply disturbed. Perhaps the excesses in the money supply and the inadequacies of the banking system, two serious current problems, can be alleviated by administrative measures. However, inflation is likely to remain troublesome. And there is a broader, more difficult issue with political as well as economic implications. Regionalism, implicit in the current economic policies, is once again a rising challenge to national unity. Indeed, some Chinese speak of a new era of warlordism—three thousand economic warlords pursuing local policies down to the county level, policies that are often separate from, even in defiance of, those of the center.

Thus, unexpectedly, an old problem has reemerged. A state once defined by some as totalitarian is struggling to regain control over an economy that in many regions is operating under its own momentum and rules, ignoring or defying central instructions. In the process, semi-autonomous regional systems are emerging, of which the Guangdong–Hong Kong enclave is the most significant. The Beijing government itself has made a contribution to this development by establishing as basic policy an emphasis on economic growth in the leading portions of eastern, coastal China, with extensive reliance upon local initiatives. Since it is in these areas that some infrastructure exists or can be most easily developed, it is a sound policy economically, but it has far-reaching political and social implications, as can be readily appreciated.

A second, related problem concerns the fostering of entrepreneurship and its mode of operation. With the old private sector (such as it was) having shriveled under socialism, it is natural that new entrepreneurs are being drawn largely from the ranks of officialdom, civil and military. Senior cadres are entrusted with making money for their organizations—and also for themselves. Continuing long-established habits, they depend extensively upon political contacts and an exchange of favors. Competitiveness through enhanced efficiency is largely foreign to their culture and experience. Under such conditions corruption has mushroomed, as China in some respects returns to an old system centering on bureaucratic capitalism.

Current events in the People's Republic of China, as elsewhere in the socialist world, illustrate the fact that there is no painless method of abandoning Stalinist economics. No Leninist state has yet successfully melded the command economy and the market economy—not Yugoslavia, not Hungary (where hope once ran high), and not the Soviet Union, where the experiment is only beginning. The years immediately ahead will be difficult ones for China. Heated debate over the tempo and scope of change is certain to continue. The current evidence suggests, however, that although there will be zigzags and much slogging with no clear map in hand, the basic changes now underway are likely to continue, accompanied by an expanding interaction with external market economies, especially those of Hong Kong, Japan, South Korea, and Taiwan.

Ideological and systemic barriers to foreign economic relations are being rapidly lowered. In the battle for the mind—and the soul—of China, the pragmatism so deeply implanted in Chinese culture is eroding Leninism. China may well have an advantage over the USSR in this respect. As the overseas Chinese population illustrates so well, creativity and independent entrepreneurship thrive when they are liberated from political chaos and state repression. Pre-Soviet Russian culture does not provide comparative examples, suggesting that in the short term at least, the challenges confronting Gorbachev may be greater than those facing Beijing's leaders. In Russia, the time separating serfdom and agrarian collectivization was not great, and entrepreneurship had a stunted development under the czars. Nearly seven decades of Stalinist economics followed, a sufficient period to separate present generations, even the oldest, from the presocialist era. Thus, Gorbachev's task is not merely to change Soviet economic policies; it is also to change Russian culture, a goal extraordinarily difficult to achieve quickly or easily.

Reforms in the People's Republic are being undertaken in the name of socialism, this being defined as the primary stage and hence requiring the construction of socialist preconditions. But the genius of this society lies in the Chinese capacity to keep words and actions separate, so that they may serve different purposes. One cannot predict the mix that will take place among nationalized portions of the economy, joint ventures of various sorts, cooperatives, and the private sector. Whatever evolves, Chinese leaders may well continue to call it socialism with Chinese characteristics. But the real issue will be the extent to which the state should or can regulate the dynamic economic forces that have recently been set loose.

Political changes are also in China's future, but their dimensions are still uncertain. Like others, the Chinese leaders have come to realize that as one implements economic reform, the need for political reform likewise grows. One cannot encourage innovative, productive economic citizens while keeping them politically mute. The dilemma is clear: how to allow politics to evolve, yet not lose control while negotiating the slippery path of economic change. Like Mikhail Gorbachev more recently, Deng Xiaoping once found it politically useful to promote trenchant criticism of the old order. When this threatened to go beyond the bounds that governing authorities considered proper, however, Deng and his associates applied restraints. Yet as the rather lame campaign against "bourgeois liberalism" indicated, leaders must be careful to avoid the type of wholesale repression that would stifle the intellectual class and thereby damage the drive for economic revitalization. For the time being at least, the Soviet Union has gone far beyond China with respect to intellectual freedom. But in both societies, restrictions on civil rights will constantly be tested as the two governments and various local authorities make decisions as to what is useful (or, at a minimum, acceptable) and what is dangerous. Especially important will be decisions regarding the media. Recent dramatic developments, still ongoing, testify to the uncertainties that mark China's political path.

Changes are also taking place in the institutional structure of the Chinese state. First, increased competition is being allowed within the one-party system. Chinese authorities have repeatedly made it clear that they have no intention of allowing genuinely competitive parties. The dictatorship of the Communist Party must be upheld, they insist, along with the socialist system and Marxism–Leninism–Mao Zedong thought. Yet they are permitting more competition within the party, albeit generally from a pool of individuals previously cleared by party authorities. There is also evidence of greater assertiveness within the government's legislative and advisory bodies. At sessions of the National People's Congress and the People's Political Consultative Conference, the questioning of policies and the airing of complaints have increased and have been given greater publicity. After decades of ritualistic acquiescence with every government act, today there is a measure of debate. In addition, an effort has been made to separate more clearly the party and the government, giving the latter increased power to operate without interference. The implications of this division could be far-reaching, but the jurisdictional boundaries are still ill-defined.

In sum, the political atmosphere in contemporary China is significantly different from that of the 1960s and 1970s. One may assert that this nation is moving from Leninism into the authoritarian-pluralist category of societies. Indeed, it is possible to argue that in some respects, as I have noted, the authority of the party and state is being threatened; ideology is at low ebb and, even more important, control over many basic economic activities in the society is minimal or nonexistent. China's great size and diversity—together with the relaxation of economic and political controls—have once again brought into question the government's power to manage the society. Economic conditions, moreover, have produced rising discontent among the intellectual and professional classes, weakening at least temporarily the legitimacy of the system and of its leaders. In sum, the image of contemporary China as a strong state requires significant modification.

It cannot be doubted, furthermore, that since institutionalization is still weak, government remains highly personalized and succession is a major question. After Deng, what? Will it be possible to construct and maintain a genuinely collective leadership? This would be truly remarkable for a society and a system that have always required a paramount figure at the top of the political structure, a de jure or de facto emperor. Thus, China's new revolution is replete with uncertainties, but the changes underway promise to alter the society even more profoundly than those that occurred when the Chinese Communists first came to power.

A new era is also evident in foreign policy. China's current foreign policies are rooted not in ideology but in a perception of national interest, a perception extensively influenced by both nationalist and traditional sentiments. Earlier concepts of two camps and subsequently of three worlds have been abandoned or significantly altered. At present, China operates in the international realm very much like other nation-states, albeit a state that is weak, in need of assistance, and above all determined to give priority to domestic development. The latter factor prompts Chinese leaders, like the leaders of other major societies today, to seek a low-cost, low-risk foreign policy. Indeed, it is precisely in this trend that one sees the most profound change in international relations in decades, perhaps in history.

China's declaration of nonalignment and its effort to identify itself politically with the Third World provide a substitute for the earlier ideological commitment to global revolution and solidarity with the socialist camp. Third World identification also contains a ring of truth, since China shares many of the problems and needs of other developing states. Yet Beijing must wrestle with a contradiction, one implicit in its size and the attitudes derived from its historic relationships with others. China is more than a backward state. It is a major state, and accepted as such by other states, especially by its smaller neighbors. Despite China's multiple weaknesses, moreover, the Chinese are used to playing the role assigned them. Even in recent times, their attitude toward others has betrayed a traditional flavor; they have accepted tribute from some "barbarians" for example, and made an effort to punish others. Furthermore, the time when the People's Republic provided assistance to Communist guerrilla movements in neighboring states is not so distant as to be forgotten. It is scarcely surprising, therefore, that despite Beijing's assurances that it wants only peaceful coexistence with states having different political systems and that it will never seek hegemony, other Asian nations continue to voice apprehensions regarding the power that China may acquire in the future.

Meanwhile, China's ability to make a distinction between words and actions has never been clearer than with respect to its two-Koreas policy. The People's Republic pays political homage to North Korea while it expands economic and cultural relations with South Korea at a phenomenal rate. North Korea is China's legal wife, but South Korea is its favorite concubine.

China's relations with the major Pacific-Asian nations further reveal the pragmatism that now governs its foreign policies. Only a decade ago, Deng and other Chinese spokesmen were calling for a global alliance headed by the United States to block Soviet hegemonism. Such a policy, however, potentially involved costs for China incompatible with its domestic goals. And the international scene was changing. The U.S. military buildup in the Pacific and elsewhere reestablished a strategic balance to Beijing's satisfaction. The Soviet Union, bogged down in Afghanistan and afflicted with aging, weak leadership, seemed less of a threat. Thus, even before the advent of Gorbachev, the Chinese proclaimed their policy to be one of nonalignment. Directing criticism at both "superpowers" on specific issues, the Chinese set forth their terms for "normalization" with the USSR and improvement of relations with the United States.

With the so-called three obstacles (border troops, Afghanistan, and Cambodia) resolved or reduced, Sino-Soviet relations are now approaching normalcy. Old polemics and threats have disappeared. Economic and cultural ties are being reconstructed, and high-level meetings between leaders are taking place. Party-to-party relations may soon be restored. Some observers note that the Soviets appear likely to borrow certain reform policies from the Chinese, reversing a pattern of earlier decades. Others claim that China is moving toward a position equidistant from both the United States and the USSR. Indeed, it is possible that in the near term China's policies will prove to be too clever by half, advancing relations with the USSR to the point where doubts and fears are raised in Japan and the United States. Yet there is one obstacle that cannot be removed: the geopolitical realities of the Eurasian continent. Two great land empires will continue to live cheek by jowl, with no significant buffer-state system to separate them. In the case of both nations, moreover, and particularly the Soviet Union, outer borders are sensitive and vulnerable because in the frontier regions population is relatively sparse, ethnic minorities predominate, and developmental problems are severe. Can genuine trust be established between Chinese and Russians under such conditions?

Meanwhile, despite recent trends and certain grievances or misgivings, China's relations with the other two major nations of the Pacific, Japan and the United States, remain considerably more substantial than those with the USSR, whether the measure be economic, cultural, or strategic. The legacy of hostility for nearly a century has not been overcome in Sino-Japanese relations. Even publicly, Chinese spokesmen comment on Japanese reluctance to share technology and on the risks of Japanese militarism or ultra-nationalism. Private sentiments are sharper. For many Chinese, sentiments toward the Japanese stop at respect; they do not extend to warmth. Yet with reason, the Chinese count upon Japan to be a principal source of support for their unfolding industrial revolution. One-fourth of all China's trade is conducted with Japan, and a substantial portion of foreign loans comes from that source, directly or indirectly.

Relations with the United States are equally important in a somewhat different sense. More than thirty thousand Chinese students are being trained in the United States at present, the overwhelming majority in science and technology. Even if the brain drain is substantial, as seems likely to be the case under present conditions, those who return to China will ultimately play key roles in their society, just as certain Soviet-trained students of the 1950s are doing today. Together with American technology, the students can provide the People's Republic with a basis for more rapid advancement, if they are properly utilized. To this must be added the limited but meaningful strategic relations that have developed between the two countries via the transfer of dual-use technology, defensive military equipment, and information exchanges.

In reality, therefore, China's current foreign policy is one of tilted nonalignment, and the tilt is toward the United States and Japan. The reason is at once fundamental and simple. Only the latter two nations can at present play the critical roles in advancing those goals which every nation seeks: security and development. Notwithstanding such issues as Taiwan and trade, moreover, the tilt will continue so long as Beijing believes that the relationships are serving these critical needs.

THE OTHER LENINIST societies of Asia present a different picture, but here, too, changes are at hand. North Korea illustrates most powerfully the compatibility between traditionalism and Leninism in its Asian setting. At the apex of the political system stands an aging god-king whose authority is unchallengeable. Yet over him hangs the shadow of Stalin and Mao, two other men who, though virtually deified during their lives, could not control events from their graves. The issue of succession looms large, and knowledgeable opinions about Kim Il-song's son and heir-apparent are shaded with doubts. It would be extraordinary if there were a placid, uneventful transition from Kim Il-song's reign to a new era, irrespective of the talents—or lack thereof—of his son. The old order, kept intact by Kim and his associates, has been based upon xenophobic nationalism, a truly primitive cult of personality, the protection of the masses from outside contamination, and Stalinist economics preserved with very limited change.

Such a system belongs almost certainly to the past, not to the future. Already there are stirrings among the younger, better-educated elite, and mounting external pressures from the DPRK's two big socialist allies. Most important, the North has lost the economic competition with the South, and sooner or later it must adjust to that fact. Today, North Korea faces declining productivity, plant obsolescence, food shortages, and a foreign debt in default. Its GNP is only about one-fifth that of the South, although it has one-half the South's population. Never were the shortcomings of an autarkic economy more evident.

Timid efforts in the direction of economic change have begun. The government has enacted a joint-venture law and has made appeals for investment from Koreans living in Japan. It also looks longingly toward Japan in broader terms. But there is little about the North Korean economy at present that would attract foreign capital, and DPRK commodities that can generate foreign exchange are very scarce. North Korea's principal exchange earnings at present appear to come from military sales.

Economic logic would dictate the development of intercourse with the South, where capital and technology exist in abundance. And this appears to be underway, although political obstacles make progress difficult. The course of North-South discussions over nearly two decades has been extremely rocky, as intermittent dialogue has been interrupted by lengthy periods of rigid hostility. Historically, the South has given priority to economic and cultural exchanges, postponing political and military agreements until a network of other ties enabling trust could be built. The North has insisted first of all on political and military measures that would lead to the removal of American forces from the South and create a confederated state—a North Korean version of the Chinese "one country/two systems" formula.

Recently, the Roh Tae Woo administration signaled its willingness to explore political as well as economic agreements with the North, and various probings are underway. Yet the possibility of a reunified Korea seems remote. The gulf between the two states and societies is enormous, and growing. Can North Korea's government take the risk of allowing its people broad access to the South? Almost certainly, Pyongyang will seek to use united-front tactics in dealing with Seoul, taking advantage of the pluralism existing there to draw some elements to its side. And whatever the results of such a tactic, the challenge to internal stability in both South and North remains a critical variable. Peaceful coexistence and the onset of beneficial cross-contacts require a reasonably stable atmosphere in both Koreas. Any upheaval will heighten the temptation either to await the outcome or possibly to shape it.

Meantime, North Korean foreign policy in its broader dimensions is in flux. Pyongyang proclaims itself nonaligned in the international arena, although its dependence upon Soviet assistance has risen sharply. In reality, North Korea has rarely if ever been equidistant from both China and Russia; rather, it has tilted first in one direction, then in the other, as needs and circumstances have dictated. To be sure, since the Korean War, it has refused to align itself totally with either big Communist state so as to avoid deeply antagonizing the other. And like some other states, since the late 1950s it has been able to take advantage of the Sino-Soviet split to play one country off against the other.

Thus, Sino-Soviet rapprochement is of concern to North Korea, the more so because both major socialist states are at present showing a strong interest in South Korea, despite

Pyongyang's protests. As a possible augury of things to come, Hungary has established a political relationship with South Korea to underwrite its economic and cultural ties with that nation. In the Third World, too, the North Korean position has slipped after significant gains in the 1960s. The DPRK's repeated resort to terrorism and the continuing high ideological quotient in its foreign policy have rendered the country more isolated in the international community than at any time in its forty-year history.

It is therefore logical that North Korea should seek new policies, foreign as well as domestic, and there are certain signs that it is in fact doing so; but the effort is being made hesitantly and is accompanied by differences of opinion. The obvious targets are Japan and the United States. Current goals with respect to the former are to secure economic assistance and to broaden informal political contacts. From the latter, North Korea hopes to obtain some form of recognition that might possibly lead to official negotiations on troop withdrawal. In these aims, Pyongyang enjoys strong support from both Moscow and Beijing, since such developments help them legitimize their contacts with Seoul, and might also serve to reduce tensions on the Korean peninsula. Unless there is some radical change of circumstances, cross-contacts with both Koreas by the major states are bound to grow; the only questions concern timing and extent. If these expanded contacts can be coupled with productive North-South negotiations, the prospects for a more stable peace will become stronger.

To the northwest, the Mongolian People's Republic is a somewhat less tense society, having lived under a Soviet system—and Russian protection—for more than sixty years. Yet here, too, the price of Leninism has been rising. The old political system—including the apparatus of a police state—remains essentially intact, symbolized by the statue of Joseph

Stalin that still stands in front of the Mongolian Academy of Sciences. The one asset is a better-educated elite. The economy is backward and in trouble. Yet one increasingly hears the voice of a younger generation, more highly educated and eager to explore the outer world. These individuals welcome the recent ties established with the United States and cherish the hope that Gorbachev's efforts will prove successful, thereby influencing events in Mongolia. It is significant that in 1988 the government instituted a number of economic reforms resembling those earlier introduced in China.

In Mongolia, too, nationalism is a potent factor, despite or perhaps because of the strong Soviet influence. The Mongols take pride in their history and traditions. The USSR, however, will remain the dominant external power because, as I have indicated, it alone is a credible defender of the Mongols against any possible Chinese expansion. In foreign policy, Mongolia's options are few, given the country's geopolitical circumstances. At one time the Japanese empire reached to its doorstep, but that era seems quite distant today. Its only massive neighbor is China, which as late as the 1920s counted Mongolia as part of its empire. Some Mongols worry that that claim may be reasserted in the twenty-first century.

The most recent Leninist states of Asia are the three nations of Indochina, and here the central actor is Vietnam. No one would presumably challenge the assertion that this society has been in deep trouble in recent years. The seriousness of the situation was graphically illustrated by the slogan adopted by the Sixth Vietnam Workers Party Congress in December 1986: "Renewal or death." Renewal referred to the need to find some way back to the Communist ideals of cadre purity and economic dynamism, ideals which now represent a cruel mockery of earlier dreams. At the Sixth Congress and at other official meetings, it was acknowledged that economic conditions in Vietnam were deplorable and that some provinces were suffering near-starvation. In 1975, when the victorious Communists rode into Saigon on trucks and tanks, few would have imagined that in a little over a decade Hanoi would be imploring the international community for assistance in obtaining necessities, despite massive Soviet aid.

Beginning in 1987 the new secretary-general of the Workers Party, Nguyen Van Linh, called for sweeping reforms, policy changes bearing some relation to Chinese and Soviet reforms. These were designed to expand opportunities for private initiative, to relax internal trade restrictions and other impediments to commerce, and to encourage foreign investment and trade. Accompanying the economic breakdown has been massive corruption affecting every branch of society, including some of the highest party figures. In successive drives in the recent past, thousands of cadres have been purged from the party, but there is no evidence that this has significantly alleviated the problem. It is both systemic and a product of the desperate nature of conditions.

As might have been expected, the steady worsening of the economic situation ultimately found political expression— once again, largely among the political elite. Criticisms poured forth at party meetings, including the Sixth Congress. A number of first-line veterans were retired, various self-criticisms were issued, and some political reforms were instituted. Progressives urged greater participation by the citizenry; the government permitted more meaningful competition for key posts and, within limits, allowed candid discussion of current problems. Leaders were clearly worried about the people's loss of confidence in the party and government. Thus, the drive for "democratization" was combined with a promise to rid the party of "bullies" and immoral elements.

Will it be possible for Linh, who was seventy-three in 1988, and a few senior associates to turn the tide? Will they be able to enlist support from some of the tens of thousands of Soviet-trained, younger Vietnamese? And amid continuing conservative opposition from many cadres, including the highest, will they be able to carry out the reforms essential if public support is to be achieved? Indeed, does anyone know what combination of reforms will work for socialist Vietnam—or other Leninist societies of similar type?

Vietnamese leaders are watching Gorbachev's efforts with great interest. Soviet policies have generally had a strong influence on the Vietnamese, even in the days of Stalin. And undoubtedly, the Soviets' advice that North Vietnam show flexibility in reaching a political solution with respect to Cambodia bolsters Hanoi's realization that its heavy military expenditures in that campaign, together with the need for huge forces to guard the northern frontier with China, contribute mightily to the nation's economic troubles.

Even more than North Korea, Vietnam has reason to be concerned about Sino-Soviet rapprochement, since China remains a stubborn opponent and the Russians have let it be known they are deeply disturbed that their aid has been squandered through Vietnamese mismanagement. Hanoi realizes that at some point it must reach an accommodation with the Chinese, unless it chooses to be reconciled to extensive militarization, permanent poverty, and dependence on some external power. It has therefore renewed its dialogue with China. In the meantime, Vietnam is seeking almost desperately to open windows to the nonsocialist world, especially to the United States and Japan. Given current trends within the socialist community, the small socialists see that their self-interest lies in expanding their contacts, especially with the advanced industrial nations.

LET ME NOW summarize the broad trends characterizing Asia's Leninist states today—trends likely to shape the future. Shortly after World War II, the theory of convergence enjoyed a certain vogue. Put simply, this theory held that in liberal societies the state would become more involved in economic management and social services, while socialist states would relax their political controls. The two would thus meet in the vicinity of social democracy. In the light of events, present and projected, that theory requires significant modification. There is no reason to believe that we shall see the emergence of a universal identity among societies so different in culture, stage of development, human and natural resources, and geopolitical circumstances. And if the developmental process will narrow certain gaps, it may widen others or even invert certain relationships between countries. At present, for example, most advanced industrial nations are moving toward privatization rather than toward increased statism. Social democracy, having achieved a certain status, is currently on the defensive, although various safety nets are not likely to be removed.

The Leninist states are moving not toward liberalism but toward variations of the authoritarian-pluralist model, a model characteristic of the earlier stages of the most successful developing societies. As we have noted, this trend is powerfully abetted by the inadequacy of Stalinist economies at this point in the developmental process. In Asia, China leads the way, while Vietnam hobbles along at the beginning of the path. North Korea and Mongolia bring up the rear, but the time when autarkic economies based on mobilization tactics can meet the minimal requirements of these societies is drawing to a close. The only questions are when and how changes will come. Yet, as I have emphasized, the challenge of imposing a new economic strategy upon a tenacious Stalinist framework remains formidable; hence, recurrent instability is a virtual certainty in the years ahead.

In contrast to earlier times, today economics is in command, and politics is the dependent variable. Political change starts with the rusting of ideology, as pragmatic experimentation comes to the fore. Interacting with this is the demythologizing of the past, including those individuals once labeled as supermen. These developments have profound consequences. Throughout the Leninist world (with North Korea possibly excepted for the time being), there is a crisis of belief. Never again can Leninist regimes count on the type of conformity that existed in the past. And modern exercises in greater political openness and in limited political competition, while proceeding unevenly and subject to potential reversals, are reducing the gap between the inner thoughts and desires of the citizenry and the pageantry of public politics. This gap often resulted in a unique combination of ritualistic participation and political lethargy at the mass level. Once, citizens in Leninist states were organized so that they would be pliant consumers of whatever orthodoxy was being dispensed. Now they are becoming more truly politicized. In the future, political legitimacy in socialist societies will hinge increasingly on the effectiveness of developmental measures in improving the life of the common man. "Am I better off?"—the litmus test of democratic regimes—is a question spreading to Leninist societies.

Developments in foreign policy are attuned to domestic trends. Nationalism—and the perception of national interest—overwhelmed socialist idealism long ago. The fact that two countries may be ideologically compatible and may share similar institutions is insufficient to ensure amity in the socialist world. At present we witness the widest spectrum of relations among and between Leninist states—a pattern ranging from alliance to hostility, and one that is indistinguishable from that of other types of states. Internationalism in its more dynamic forms is being advanced not through the brotherhood of the global proletariat but via participation in the market-oriented regional and international economic order. It is an internationalism bearing scant relation to that envisaged by Marxist-Leninist pioneers, but potentially more profound. Meanwhile, the major Leninist states, in company with others, are committed to a less adventurous foreign policy so as to heighten the priorities on domestic reform. In this, one sees great hope for fostering genuine peaceful coexistence.

Taking these developments into account, it is reasonable to assert that we are witnessing the opening stages of a seismic change in the major Leninist societies, a change that—whatever reverses may be encountered—does indeed warrant being designated a revolution. It is a development, moreover, that is inextricably connected with the ongoing global revolution triggered by new scientific and technological advances affecting all political-economic systems. The central issue in the coming decades will concern the adjustments that each system must make to adapt itself to the prevailing tides of change. If the changes required of the Leninist system are more profound than those required of other systems (as I believe they will be), then the revolution in Leninist societies will be more intense.

THE CULTURAL, structural, and policy differences among the authoritarian-pluralist states of Asia make generalizations regarding economic strategies and their results hazardous and subject to various caveats. Nevertheless, one can discern certain broad patterns. Initial policies supported import substitution and government intervention on behalf of domestic producers. Where relatively high growth rates were sustained, such as in the NICs (Newly Industrialized Countries), now frequently labeled NIEs (Newly Industrialized Economies)—namely South Korea, Taiwan, Hong Kong, and Singapore—a combination of domestic savings and foreign loans were available in ample supply and effectively invested. This strategy may be said to have laid the foundations for accelerated growth, but it also resulted in deficiencies similar to some of those characterizing the economies of the Leninist states. Continual trade deficits and balance-of-payment problems produced a rising national debt and retarded growth. Inefficiency was rife, sheltered by protectionism. Consequently, administrations initiated new policies centered on export orientation. A gradual relaxation of governmental controls took place, as the private sector was given greater flexibility. Trade liberalization accompanied this trend. Measures to attract foreign investment were inaugurated. These measures harmonized with the desire of the advanced industrial nations to internationalize their production so as to take advantage of lower labor costs and reduce the protectionist threat.

It has been this basic strategy that has underwritten the phenomenal success of such economies as those of South Korea and Taiwan. Structural differences among the NIEs, to be sure, have existed. South Korea has fostered the growth of large conglomerates similar to the prewar Japanese *zaibatsu*. Taiwan's small and medium-sized enterprises have made the accumulation of private funds for research and development more difficult. Nonetheless, both societies have taken maximum advantage of the international environment to advance rapidly toward higher technology production, as part of an increasingly integrated regional market. Indeed, the NIEs are now playing a vital role as a third leg in a new and dynamic economic triangle, absorbing more U.S. imports and significantly raising their exports to Japan.

The economic development of most South and Southeast Asian societies has been beset with greater difficulties. Resource-rich in certain cases, they have been more strongly dependent upon the sale of primary products on the international market, and hence have been at the mercy of fluctuating prices for such commodities. Yet one can see in these countries some of the same broad trends that are found in the NIEs: the shift in emphasis from import substitution to export promotion, with stress on agro-industrial processing; increased reliance upon the private sector, and relaxation of governmental controls; trade liberalization, along with an effort to reduce dependence on foreign loans; and heightened measures to attract foreign investment and technology transfer.

Where these adjustments have been most successfully made, such as in Thailand, growth rates are rising. It is likely that soon there will be additional NIEs. In states such as Bangladesh, where population-resource factors are strongly adverse, or where the removal of bureaucratic obstacles is retarded, such as in India, development is hampered. It should be noted, however, that in India as in many similar situations, an enormous second economy thrives, outside official control. Excessively protectionist policies combined with political malfeasance may also intervene, such as in the Philippines. But broadly speaking, the Pacific-Asian region, and notably East Asia, has set the economic pace and provided lessons from which other developing societies may learn.

The essence of the evolving East Asian economic system lies in the shifting comparative advantage characterizing societies as they move from one developmental stage to another. This provides the foundation for a regionally based horizontal division of labor that replaces the old vertical structure. Societies in the forefront of the developmental process specialize in high value-added exports while cooperating in the supply of capital and technology to less-developed economies. Production is increasingly the composite result of various countries' imports, which depend on their position in the developmental scale. Meanwhile the NIEs, coming just behind the front-runners, are rapidly upgrading their production, moving into more advanced stages, and have themselves become investors in states like the members of ASEAN (Association of Southeast Asian Nations). Many of the latter states in turn represent the next generation of NIEs, accelerating their efforts to advance beyond a competition with low-labor-cost nations like China and India.

Interdependence has its hazards. The health of the global economy and, most important, of the two economic superpowers, the United States and Japan, is of the utmost importance. The sovereignty of even the most powerful nations can be compromised. Yet institutions sufficient to govern regional and global economic relations are lacking, and nations depend heavily upon summit meetings and piecemeal bilateral and multilateral agreements that are sometimes in actual or potential conflict with each other. Experience, however, has shown that there is no satisfactory alternative to the broad developmental course now underway. The challenge is to refine and modify that course as circumstances require and to create or improve the institutions necessary to manage it, while seeking to prepare for its profound social and political consequences.

THESE CONSEQUENCES can already be seen in societies like South Korea and Taiwan, two authoritarian-pluralist states now in the midst of a major political transition. Unlike the political revolution in Leninist states, the revolution underway in these societies is the product of success, not failure.

Furthermore, it is a revolution generated at least partly from below, not one initiated wholly by political elites. The rapid expansion of more literate, more affluent, more urban "middle classes" provides the foundation for greater political openness and more genuine participation in the political process. The term "middle class," incidentally, is inappropriate if understood in its classic Western sense. The vanguard agitating for a new politics consists primarily of students, intellectuals, journalists, and assorted professional elements. The commercial-business class, disillusioned with the government's policies or its capacity to retain the allegiance of the citizenry, may join or support the political reformers, but this class remains strongly concerned about stability and seeks in many cases to direct governmental power on its behalf rather than allowing a reduction in that power.

The authoritarian-pluralist state is susceptible to political change not merely because of today's socioeconomic currents but also because its leaders are themselves pledged to political evolution. Unlike Leninist power holders, they do not claim to have established political institutions in final form, or to have fixed the boundaries of legal political behavior for all time. On the contrary, in one way or another they have repeatedly declared that as their society reaches a more advanced stage of growth, political change can and should occur. Thus, Chun Doo Hwan often asserted that he would be the first Korean president to leave office by means of a competitive national election. Chiang Ching-kuo indicated that Taiwan was ready to accept a quasi-legal opposition and other political measures that would clearly require significant alterations in the old system. In Thailand, Prime Minister Prem Tinsulanoud stepped down voluntarily and named as his successor an elected member of parliament capable of presiding over a majority coalition, albeit a man with a military as well as a business background. To be sure, broad socioeconomic and political events nudged, pushed, perhaps forced these leaders in the direction they took. But their actions were in accord with the type of legitimacy that they sought and with the promises, direct or indirect, that they had made.

In two authoritarian-pluralist Asian societies of recent times, the scenario differed from that which I have outlined. In the Philippines, after a promising start, Ferdinand Marcos presided over deepening failures, brought on by political and economic mismanagement. Only a spark was necessary to inflame the people, and that came in the form of Benigno Aquino's assassination. But here, too, the political revolt was led by outraged elements of the Filipino "middle class," aided by the Catholic hierarchy and the split within the military at the climatic moment. Burma, the other exception to the scenario, has been closer to the classic Leninist model than to authoritarian-pluralism. Rigorous repression and extreme autarky in both the political and economic realms left the society in near-total collapse. It appeared as if the military leadership had consciously adopted stagnation as a strategy for stability. When revolt came, it was from the students, joined by monks, white-collar workers, and assorted others—roughly equivalent to what remained of Burma's "middle class." Largely leaderless and without arms, they continue to fight toward an uncertain end against a military that may retain its strength and coercive capacity if it can preserve its own unity. Political reform has been promised, but the immediate future is murky. Sooner or later, however, Burma seems certain to join in the regional trend taking place around it.

This development signals yet another powerful force of this era—namely, the communications-information revolution that makes it increasingly difficult to isolate the people of any society, and particularly their more articulate elements, from regional and global events. An awareness of events in the Philippines entered the political pores of South Korea at a critical point. The legacy of both these countries, and the wholly different prospects that lie ahead for Thailand, are a part of the consciousness of the Burmese rebels. One may properly speak of a domino factor in this sense.

While the general trend toward democratization in Asia's authoritarian-pluralist societies is apparent to all, one cannot ignore the political fragility of many of the states undergoing such a transition and the difficulty of institutionalizing the new system. Western-style parliamentarism, even when modified to accord with certain cultural imperatives, is so different from key traditions that the transition to this style of government is bound to be hazardous. As indicated earlier, Asia has always been reluctant to recognize the individual as a separate entity; communalism of various types forms the basis of Asian culture. Translated into political terms, this supports respect for authority, legitimacy based on status rather than accomplishments, dependence upon patron-client relations, and consensus as a method of decision making. Given this last commitment, tolerance toward one's opponents is often minimal, since they are presumed to stand outside the legitimate process and since majoritarianism is of questionable validity. Yet one of the indispensable rules of the parliamentary game is that one must not treat the opposition as the enemy, eligible for annihilation. Opponents of the government must not move with abandon from the legislative halls to the streets, calling for the death of those in power. And the government must not rid itself of opponents by censoring, imprisoning, or killing them unless they defy the democratic system itself through open rebellion. These lessons were learned with difficulty in the West over centuries, and in Japan over a number of decades. Can the learning process be shortened for societies like South Korea, Taiwan, Thailand,

and Indonesia? And can the Philippines, in the midst of serious social fissures and economic trouble—with the gap between the society and the system as great as ever—legitimize the democratic order, even one that has been a vital part of its past?

One must be especially concerned about two groups at once critical to the initiation of democracy and potentially its ultimate enemies: the students and the media. The students, ardently opposed to the old order and bravely leading the charge, are susceptible to a false idealism and to being led unwittingly in an antidemocratic direction that insists upon a monopoly of truth and defies democratic procedures. Exhilarated by early victories, they may also seek to perpetuate organization—and their own importance on the political scene—at any cost, searching desperately for issues that will serve this purpose, even issues with scant merit. The more radical South Korean students epitomize this hazard. And the media, by sensationalizing events and trivializing serious policy issues, can influence and even force political figures to adhere to their standards, in the process making the citizens increasingly cynical or indifferent. If mature democratic societies have not found solutions to these problems, especially the problem of the media, there is no reason to believe that success will come easily to young democracies.

Some of the above problems become more acute when political openness threatens to widen long-existing racial, religious, or regional cleavages. Even in such a homogeneous society as South Korea, strong regional antagonisms were revealed in the 1987 elections, and some candidates catered to these sentiments. The issue in Taiwan is more delicate, given the historic animosity between many Taiwanese and the citizens who came as refugees from the mainland. In southern Asia, the well-known racial-ethnic and religious divisions coupled with the rivalries of diverse regions have long been sources of political instability. There is a fine line between the right of interest groups in a democracy to express their political views and the use of an open political forum to intensify racial, religious, and regional tensions, in the process delegitimizing both the system and the state. Long ago, it was asserted in the U.S. Supreme Court that one should not be allowed to shout "Fire!" in a crowded theater. But the issue remains controversial, and the line is often obscured in the older democratic states. One cannot expect that it will be maintained easily in new democracies. Ethnicity is the one permanent factor in the politics of any society, and an adjustment to that fact is a task never fully accomplished.

In these various matters, leadership remains a supremely important variable. If the transition involves a move from military to civilian rule, as is often the case, the challenge may be all the more complex. In addition to the fact that new institutions must be created, modes of behavior must also be altered. The art of democratic politics is not the same as that of military politics, although there are links between them. Every society makes unique cultural demands upon its leaders, and no single set of qualifications applies universally. However, effective political leadership in societies moving from authoritarianism to parliamentarism requires a mix of flexibility and firmness that needs frequent readjustment, a keen sense of timing, an ability to build coalitions from diverse elements, a capacity to garner and retain able advisors, and the skill—and luck—to develop policies that accord with rapidly evolving domestic and international requirements. This transitional period is not a time for amateurs, however well-meaning. In the initial stages particularly, a leader establishes his or her image, and sets in motion a political style that deeply influences subsequent events. It is not without reason that we carefully watch the actions of individuals like Roh Tae Woo and Lee Teng-hui, and are concerned about Corazon Aquino.

There is nothing inevitable or necessarily irreversible about any political trend. Some of the democracies that are evolving out of authoritarian states may succumb, as happened shortly after World War II. Yet the world has changed since the 1950s, and these societies with it. We now understand, however, that the interrelation between politics and economics is neither predetermined nor identical. One common trend is taking place. We are witnessing the politicization of the masses across all political systems in a form and to a degree hitherto unknown. If authoritarianism does reemerge, it must take account of this fact. It cannot simply restore the past. On balance, however, the odds favor continued experimentation with political as well as socioeconomic pluralism among the authoritarian-pluralist category of states.

THE FOREIGN POLICIES of such states, like those of the Leninist nations, are being increasingly shaped by economic considerations. Formerly, one could discern two broad policies: alliance and "neutralism" (or "nonalignment"). Alliance has been practiced predominantly with the United States and has been a policy of South Korea, the Philippines, Thailand, and Pakistan. The leading nonaligned states have been Indonesia, Malaysia, and Burma, as well as the majority of South Asian states. But a combination of economic, strategic, and political factors are profoundly altering both of these earlier alternatives. Alliances are becoming alignments. The earlier close, all-encompassing ties, whereby the senior partner pledged strong security and economic assistance and the junior partner promised virtually unconditional political allegiance, are in the process of changing. In today's complex environment, in which the nature of power is being reshaped and domestic concerns are assuming higher priority, the guarantees of the so-called superpowers are more limited and more conditioned. And with the rise of self-confidence in the junior partners has come a surge of nationalism, with gestures of self-assertion on various issues, sometimes in opposition to the patron country. For the United States, as for the Soviet Union, the management of alignments has become a supreme diplomatic and strategic challenge.

At the same time, nonalignment, though still widely proclaimed and very useful politically, is a concept increasingly at odds with reality. When neutralism was in vogue some decades ago, it meant that an Asian state was declaring its independence from either of the two power blocs, or proclaiming that it was equidistant from those blocs. Its successor, nonalignment, was also based on the concept of independent policies informed by calculations of national interest; but nonaligned nations made no effort to achieve equidistance, and assumed a more active internationalist stance. Yet both of these doctrines were feasible in part because most of the developing states had not yet developed complex economic ties with any regional or international system. Such economies tended to be relatively self-sustaining and primitive. This is no longer the case. At present and for the foreseeable future, the developing states, including those I have labeled authoritarian-pluralist, are being drawn ever more closely into regional and international economic systems. And such a development has clear political and strategic implications. The one truly nonaligned nation, Burma, could protect that status only through extreme economic autarky and political isolation—and it is now in the throes of upheaval and change, as I have noted.

The foreign policies of Asia's contemporary authoritarian-pluralist states, moreover, are decidedly less prone to the type of political idealism and ideological fervor that often influenced the policies of first-generation leaders. Hence, foreign adventurism like that sponsored by Sukarno and lofty moralistic principles of the type favored by Nehru and U Nu are being replaced by developmentally oriented efforts, with foreign policies shaped to that end. Nationalism, to be sure, remains a powerful force, especially at elitist levels, and it is often used as an instrument to support greater self-assertion as interdependence grows. Security considerations are also vital concerns in certain settings, having played an especially significant role in the evolution of ASEAN and in the attitudes of all smaller states regarding the major powers. But generally speaking, the economic, developmental quotient in the foreign policies of the authoritarian-pluralist states has risen, and the ideological-political quotient has declined.

I NEXT TURN to Asia's older democracies—if one can apply that term to states that have held this status for only some four decades. In addition to Japan and India, two states differing radically in size, culture, and stage of development, we can include Malaysia, Singapore, and Sri Lanka in this category. Since these societies have never shared a common level of economic development, one cannot ascribe their political system primarily to economic factors. Moreover, the traditional cultures of these societies, whatever elements in them may have supported modernization, were patently different from each other and sufficiently foreign to democratic values to rule culture out as the wellspring of Asian democracy.

It is important to note that four of these five societies were formerly British colonies and that the other, Japan, underwent a brief but intensive period of American tutelage. As I noted earlier, British training of colonial elites, though far from uniform in its results, demonstrated a remarkable capacity to implant in certain elites political values different from those that accorded with the proclivities of their society. Furthermore, even if economic development was not the precursor of democracy in a majority of these societies, it became democracy's companion in most if not all of these cases. Singapore and Malaysia, despite a record that has had its weak points, have achieved strong growth over the past several decades. Both societies are now pursuing basically rational economic policies, correcting earlier mistakes, encouraging foreign investment and technology transfer, and taking advantage of favorable international conditions, including the upturn in prices for primary commodities. Sri Lanka, after an early overdose of state intervention, moved toward viable economic policies and was doing well until political instability intervened in the form of the Tamil separatist movement.

In contrast, India's growth according to official measures has been respectable but far from exciting, testimony to a type of quasi-socialism that falls between two stools. The government's strategy was neither sufficiently planned and effective to mobilize resources on behalf of a well-rounded infrastructure at an early point in the take-off stage, nor sufficiently open to encourage a vigorous private sector. On the surface, one still sees a tangle of bureaucratic restrictions together with various forms of protectionism. At another, unrecorded level, however, a vibrant second economy operates largely oblivious to the state, rendering Indian official statistics dubious and spurring highly differentiated regional development. In the future, the Indian economy will almost surely become more liberal, pursuing its thrust toward higher technology and toward progressive involvement with economies outside the subcontinent, notably Japan.

Indian democracy continues to survive multiple problems, defying the pessimists. Now, with nearly a half-century of experience, and a consensus in support of parliamentarism across the broadest possible political spectrum, it will not be easy to overthrow the democratic system. Supporting this system has been a federal structure that harbors a dominant national party and vigorous regional or state parties. This has encouraged political responsibility at various levels. On the negative side of the ledger is a decline in the vitality and leadership of the Congress Party. In Rajiv Gandhi, unfortunately, India has a well-meaning but unsure amateur who has thus far been unable to rebuild his party or to implement the new policies India so badly needs. Thus, much may depend upon the regional administrations and on the country's vital second economy. India shows that the relative weakness of the center may not be a disaster.

THE OTHER GREAT Asian democracy, with its own unique features, is Japan. The basic structure of the Japanese economy and its performance in the post-1945 era was discussed earlier and requires no further elucidation. Today, Japan stands astride the global economy like a modern colossus, with one foot planted in Asia, the other in the industrialized West. The central economic tasks confronting Japan are twofold and closely interrelated. It must continue the process of altering the structure of its economy, with its focus on the high-technology frontiers and the service fields. The domestic market must be greatly expanded, a development requiring major internal reforms and innovations. At the same time, Japan must become genuinely internationalist in attitudes and politics. Despite the significant advances of the recent past, the Japanese economy remains unduly exclusivist, with foreign access far more limited than in the case of the other economic superpower, the United States. This can be demonstrated by Japan's relatively low level of intraindustry trade and by a host of other factors. Protectionism—mainly in concealed forms—remains embedded in the system.

Hence the widespread feeling in the world that Japan has been selfish, taking from the international economic order far more than it has contributed. Recent governmental actions together with the appreciation of the yen have accelerated the process of change, offering hope for the future. And quite clearly the problems do not all lie with Japan. The macro-economic tasks facing the United States are formidable indeed. Yet if Japan is to develop a harmonious, constructive relation with the rest of the world, the hierarchical, corporate, inward-focused structure of the society must be altered to make possible greater openness, reciprocity, communication, and partnership. These are the forms of democratization that have genuine meaning at the international level. One must reject the argument that the cultural as well as economic changes required for such developments are too great to be expected. Rapid cultural change is an inextricable aspect of the era in which we live, especially within the avant-garde societies. In this age, one must avoid an epitaph that reads, "Too little, too late." A spirit of international participation and cooperation is essential, and, to this end, Japanese education, governmental policy, and enterprise consciousness must be mobilized with the same vigor that promoted the policies of economic nationalism in the past.

Whether the internal democratization of Japanese politics now underway will hinder or help this task is a complex question. The evolution of Japanese democracy is taking its own special course. The requisite freedoms have existed since World War II, together with the full rights of political participation and choice. Yet the combination of a dominant-party system and the extensive power of the civil service has led some observers to define Japan as a bureaucratic corporative state. Today the political role of private-interest groups is increasing, although in some sectors—such as business and agriculture—it has always been substantial.

A new breed of professional politicians is emerging, more attentive to constituent interests. Meanwhile, within the factions of the dominant Liberal Democratic Party, decision making is increasingly shared rather than being the province of a single leader. In sum, political pluralism in Japan is assuming forms different from those it has adopted in authoritarian-pluralist societies. One important issue is how to prevent democratization in these forms from retarding internationalization. Special interests frequently serve as the leading opponents of economic liberalization.

As noted earlier, another issue generic to every democracy is the role of increasingly powerful media that are free of all restraints and that possess a very limited sense of responsibility for their political impact on the society at large. This problem has grown ever more serious with the advent of television. Japan, though not representative of the problem in its most acute form, does not remain immune.

The course of the new Japanese nationalism is also a frequently discussed matter. Nationalism, it should be emphasized, is not the exclusive prerogative of developing nations. Has success—combined with the various continuing strictures placed on Japan in the international arena—revived feelings of arrogance and resentment and, at the same time, encouraged an avoidance of responsibility? Are Japanese attitudes of racial and cultural superiority being rekindled? One can certainly see evidence of such sentiments. Indeed, they have been voiced publicly by leading Japanese political figures.

However, the specter of a resurgent ultranationalism leading to an increased Japanese commitment to militarism is exaggerated. Japan has achieved a broad foreign policy consensus in recent years on the basis of a low-level defense commitment. Polls show that a strong majority of citizens support the Self-Defense Force as it exists, but do not desire a more visible or powerful force. It may be argued that Japanese military expenditures are now the world's third highest and have resulted in a small but extremely effective conventional force. Some observers also assert that as it stands today, the Japanese military force is the sixth, seventh, or eighth most formidable defense structure in the world (the assessments vary). No precise comparison is possible, and one should calculate capacity principally in relation to the military role regarded as essential to defense needs. In any case, the present Japanese Self-Defense Force is almost wholly oriented toward defense, having no aircraft carriers, long-range missiles, or other weapons of an essentially offensive nature. Moreover, it is not yet prepared to fully carry out the air and sea surveillance tasks to which it is pledged. And there are strong indications that the sentiments of a majority of the Japanese people—including the elites—will keep the Japanese military force in its present mold. Japanese leaders are well aware of the apprehensions of other Asians and go to great lengths to reassure them of Japan's modest military objectives; they are not likely to jeopardize economic advantages by military activism. And most important, the Asia of the 1980s is not the Asia of the 1930s. There is no vacuum of power on the continent, no Japanese empire to defend, and no Western-controlled colonies to liberate.

The debate over whether Japan is becoming a major military power, however, raises a much broader issue. Some analysts, their minds focused on the past, insist that military power inevitably follows economic power, and that Japan will thus move inescapably in that direction. But are we not living in a time when the balance of factors comprising power (the capacity to influence or control outcomes considered important) is undergoing a major change? And in speaking of that element of power that is military, must we not appreciate both the potentialities and the constraints that accompany its application in this era? If individuals can observe such developments, is there any reason they will not be encompassed in national policies?

Let us consider the most salient facts. On the one hand, peace at the summit—between the two nations with a global reach—has been maintained by a strategy resting upon nuclear deterrence, which has made the prospect of victory in a superpower war inconceivable. On the other hand, it has been impossible—for many reasons—to fully apply this unprecedented power to lower-level conflicts, especially those involving irregular forces. This has had two principal consequences. First, various means have been developed to avoid, limit, or camouflage direct involvement on the part of major powers in regional or localized conflicts; these means include arms transfers, support for indigenous guerrillas, the use of mercenaries or "volunteers," and the application of force short of a declared war. Second, when a major power, especially one of the two superpowers, has been directly involved, restraints have been placed on escalation. Major states have taken great pains to prevent an extension of the conflict beyond the bounds considered defensible in terms of national interests. Thus, privileged sanctuaries and external supplies to the enemy, among other handicaps, are tolerated.

It would be naïve to argue that the application of limited force by a major power, whether in its own direct interest or that of others, cannot be effective. Indeed, the important strategic shift that has begun is partly in the direction of highly sophisticated conventional weaponry attuned to mobile, rapid-response operations of a limited nature, together with more effective (and very expensive) defensive strategies to be applied at home. Yet one cannot deny that the costs and complications involved in the application of military force have significantly increased, as both the United States and the Soviet Union now recognize.

Under current global conditions, and given the trends accompanying them, how could Japan benefit from an offensive military capacity capable of being employed independently with a reasonable chance of success? Consider the possible threats to the nation from external sources. It is inconceivable that if Japan developed an independent strike capacity—nuclear or conventional—jeopardizing the Soviet Far East, the Soviets would not match it, whatever the resulting tensions in Northeast Asia. Only the alliance with the United States can provide Japan with security on this front, with the former country playing the lead role. Japan cannot hope to meet successfully any challenge from China by means of military conflict. Here, history is still valid. Indeed, given the vulnerability of Japan's strongly concentrated population and industrial facilities, to engage in a military contest with any large continental society would pose the gravest risks, and hence an aggressive military posture toward such nations would lack credibility. And whatever the level of acrimony with the United States, Japan's truly effective weapon is the economic one, as is also the case with South Korea.

It can be argued that as the Japanese economy is internationalized, Japan becomes more vulnerable to blackmail and other forms of injurious action on the part of antagonists. But such risks can rarely be countered by military power under present conditions. Indeed, this development provides an additional argument against shifting reliance to military strength. Although economic internationalization provides a powerful reason on behalf of Japan's becoming more responsible for a stable global order, the primary instrument for these purposes lies precisely in its economic power. Using that power, Japan has already demonstrated that it has the capacity to affect the policies of other nations, to influence the regional and global balance of power, and to stimulate the peace process.

It should be admitted that two events, especially if they occurred in conjunction with each other, could pose a serious dilemma for Japan. If the threat from the Soviet Union were to increase greatly, and if the United States were to engage in a precipitous military withdrawal from Asia, perceptions of security requirements within Japan would be dramatically affected. Almost certainly, opinion would be polarized, and there would be a confrontation between those favoring a much greater emphasis upon military strength and those prepared to take the neutralist-pacifist route. However, a combination of heightened Soviet threat and an American strategic withdrawal seems most unlikely.

It is likely—and desirable—that Japan will increase its political role in regional and global affairs. So long as the Japanese role is purely economic, it will be widely perceived as self-serving in the narrowest sense, despite the broader purposes being served, and in the long term it will prove unsatisfactory both for the Japanese and for others. Japan has good reason to participate in fashioning a settlement for the Arab-Israeli conflict and other tensions in the Middle East, to take more than a strictly economic role in peace-keeping activities in the aftermath of a Cambodian settlement, and to bolster those international bodies that combine economic and political functions. And with new political responsibilities must go increased authority in all organizations and international conferences, including the United Nations.

Meanwhile, the most important single tie for Japan, as for the United States, lies in their bilateral association. The apprehension concerning U.S.-Japan relations is understandable, given the severity and complexity of the problems. Theirs will be a troubled marriage in the years immediately ahead, as will the relations of each with the European Economic Community. The structural changes required on all sides are too sweeping and too swift to be painless or to permit smooth relations among those in the forefront of the revolution. But there will be no American-Japanese divorce. Economic interdependence combined with strategic dependence will keep the ties close, despite the myriad problems that attend the relationship. The economies are too thoroughly intertwined and the broad political and strategic interests too similar to allow a major cleavage. But here, as elsewhere, there will be greater independence of action within the alliance framework, and bilateral relations will be supplemented by and occasionally absorbed into multilateral arrangements (though they will also conflict with them on occasion). Meanwhile, Japan will play a leading role in the continuing internationalization of the Pacific-Asian region, including its socialist portions, sharing this role with the United States and the NIEs.

WHAT ARE THE general problems that Asia must solve in the immediate future? The two key challenges facing the Leninist societies are at once easily stated and enormously difficult to meet. First, socialist leaders must find a way to successfully revitalize ailing economies, even if this requires an abandonment of cherished dogma and a frontal assault upon entrenched power holders in the bureaucracy. Long-festering economic problems have at last caused socialist leaders to probe in the right direction. They recognize that rigid centralization is not a viable means of handling an increasingly complex, sophisticated economy. They understand that means must be found to motivate creativity and productivity at every level of the society by providing a wide range of incentives. They realize that latecomers—and all socialist states are comparative latecomers—must abandon autarky and seek entry into regional and global market networks, thereby acquiring the capital, technology, and skills necessary to accelerate the developmental process.

The leaders' acceptance of these new goals and attitudes represents an enormous advance. Naturally, there are domestic opponents—defenders of the old faith and, more important, of special interests. But the larger problem lies in creating harmony between the roles of the state and the marketplace. Formerly, the market economies of the West faced the task of applying certain regulations or restraints to the private sector in the name of social justice or economic fairness. In this process, the state increased its power and occasionally reached into the private sector in a competitive fashion, becoming owner or manager. Yet the marketplace remained essential to the system, and privatism vied with nationalization, proving itself generally the more efficient. Today many such societies are moving in the opposite direction and their governments are in retreat, although one should not underestimate the regulatory role of the state, or the need for a range of social services for every citizen.

The Leninist leaders must move their societies in a similar direction, a difficult task because in these countries the private sector has been greatly weakened by overweaning statism, and the guidelines for nurturing it are indistinct. Moreover, they are bound to encounter resistance from many of their people: the security that socialism brings continues to appeal to ordinary citizens, whatever the inadequacies of the system's economic and social results. In addition, the lack of economic improvement thus far deepens doubts at the grassroots level in some countries, such as the USSR. Furthermore, the revitalization of the private sector inevitably brings abuses, especially since many entrepreneurs must be drawn from officialdom, a class accustomed to depending on special privileges and channels of influence. The distinctions between legitimacy and corruption in the private sphere must be redrawn in a new atmosphere, and as a new entrepreneurial class emerges. These and other difficulties notwithstanding, the socialist economies must be restructured if these states are to participate more fully in the global technological revolution and compete more effectively with the market economies. The near-universal recognition of this fact, it must be reiterated, is the truly remarkable feature of our era.

The second challenge to the socialist leaders is at least equally awesome. Having accepted the importance of the marketplace with respect to goods, they are forced to accept the importance of the marketplace with respect to ideas. Greater political openness is an essential concomitant of economic restructuring. But can the Leninist system be modified in such a way as to provide the citizenry with genuine choice in the selection of those who govern, and with the degree of intellectual freedom necessary to spur new creativity in all fields? Here, too, nations are undertaking potentially far-reaching experiments. They are expanding both political competition and individual freedom—within limits. They are making efforts to separate party and government, with the aim of elevating law in the system and placing regularized procedures above personalized rule. They are tolerating, even encouraging debate—on certain issues. And most important, by means of these and other measures they are—consciously or unconsciously—shifting the test of governmental legitimacy from ideological faith to material betterment. Herein lies the real revolution: the process by which Leninism is converted from imperfect totalitarianism to an authoritarian-pluralist system founded on a developmental pattern that others have pioneered.

Meanwhile, isolation is giving way to greater intercourse with the outside world. The process of turning outward economically is being accompanied by the introduction of new information and stimuli drawn from diverse cultures. Even for those who remain at home, the electronic media furnish images of the external world which, however partial or distorted, make people realize that life elsewhere is at least different and possibly better. One story drawn from earlier times may serve to illustrate the consequences of contact with the external world, even in times of much greater repression. Some two decades ago a Chinese artist revealed that while he was watching a television film intended to depict the degradation of life in the West, what truly impressed him was the size of the rooms in a modest American home and the richness of the furnishings, in contrast to those of his own home in Hangzhou.

Those who govern socialist societies appreciate the risks of their present course. With greater freedom comes controversy and division. Leninism in its pure form brought unity, whatever the price. Outside influences can also bring "spiritual pollution," to use a recent Chinese phrase. If ideology ceases to appeal to the people and they lose faith in the party, where are the moorings for the society? What happens if the party cannot offer material improvements in sufficient degree or with some degree of equity? How does one ensure stability while experimenting with hazardous new policies? It is for these reasons that Communist leaders are loath to give up a one-party dictatorship and the immutable "truth" of Marxism-Leninism, even though they now seek to define it as a flexible, living doctrine that permits variations in societies at different stages, with different cultures. Perhaps it is not surprising, moreover, that some Chinese citizens—including young people—are talking about the need for a new ideology and a revitalized, "honest" party that will keep the faith and maintain the order necessary for economic growth. Neo-authoritarianism may have a market if chaos and corruption return.

The transition that the major Leninist societies of Eurasia

are now undergoing was triggered primarily by external developments, not by the spontaneous discoveries of internal actors, either government leaders or dissidents. The advances of the major Western industrial societies—and, even more important, the explosive dynamism of Japan and those developing states that used it as a model—stood in sharp contrast to the creeping stagnation or massive imbalances within the socialist economies. And the growing interaction among and between the market economies, despite the problems engendered, heralded a form of internationalism from which socialism was being excluded, to its great detriment.

Necessarily, the combination of new domestic priorities and the growing desire to be a part of the emerging world order has had a pronounced effect upon Leninist foreign policies. Writ large, accommodation now vies with confrontation in establishing the tone of Leninist relations, both within the socialist community and with nonsocialist states. The instinct for competition and a strong sense of national interest, including a toughness on issues deemed important, are still clearly present. Old rigidities have not totally disappeared. Yet the ideological underpinnings that contributed so mightily to that rigidity have weakened, replaced in major degree by a pragmatism that causes the Leninist foreign policies to resemble increasingly those of other nations, replete with similar stimuli, goals, and inconsistencies.

This trend presents both opportunities and problems for the nonsocialist world. The odds against a major war and in favor of a gradual process of accommodation on various fronts have grown exponentially. Yet it was relatively easy to achieve unity in the face of a rigid, ideologically driven Communism. It will be far more difficult to agree on how to handle a flexible, accommodating Communism, regarding such issues as the timing and extent of concessions or assistance.

Developments in the Soviet Union, with respect to both

domestic and foreign policy, will continue to exert great influence on other socialist states despite the progressive—and largely irreversible—growth of diversity among Leninist societies. Stretched across the Eurasian continent, the USSR will also be of crucial relevance to all its neighbors, in both the West and East, and hence to the world at large. Irrespective of the course of its domestic changes, neither the Soviet Union nor those key nations with which it interacts can escape the issues stemming from its geopolitical position. The fear of a two-front challenge—persistent throughout modern Russian history—is understandable, especially when one realizes that Moscow must defend an empire, certain parts of which have been recently acquired and are still incompletely assimilated. The current course, as I have noted, is to seek a reduction of tensions in the East through acts of withdrawal and accommodation, although the limits to such acts are clearly revealed in relations with Japan. Perhaps this will set standards for the long-term future. Perhaps the Soviet Union can establish the foundations for harmonious relations with its Asian neighbors that will serve both to eliminate the risks of large-scale conflict and to assist in the development of the Soviet Far East.

There is another scenario to be considered, however. Let us assume that China, having surmounted certain developmental problems and learned to live with others, becomes a major power in the early or mid-twenty-first century without having lost those cultural-political attributes that express themselves in a desire for recognition as a regional power, with the right to have its own buffer or tributary system. What will be the Soviet response? Meanwhile, looking at the other front, Moscow sees in the West both an opportunity and a threat. The opportunity is that it can induce Western Europe—and possibly others, including the United States—to provide the capital and technology needed to modernize the region of the USSR, namely European Russia, that already contains a considerable portion of the infrastructure necessary for rapid expansion. The threat is that the East European buffer system built at such great cost will dissolve through successive economic and political crises, posing a painful dilemma for Russian authorities and becoming a domestic political issue for Gorbachev or his successors. Perhaps here, too, the market economies can be of assistance, led by such powerful countries as West Germany. In any case, as the perception of a potential Chinese threat grows (and such a perception already exists), Soviet leaders may increasingly turn toward the West, and despite the attendant obstacles may seek to revive the old Gaullist vision of a Europe united from the Atlantic to the Urals. Naturally, the attitudes and policies of the European Economic Community, as well as the position of the United States, will be crucially important factors. It is with these broad alternatives, and their numerous permutations, that the Russian nation and people must wrestle in the decades ahead.

When one turns to that category of Asian states that I have labeled authoritarian-pluralist, one can capture for a moment the essence of the revolution which we are now experiencing. Certain societies of this group are currently feeling the full momentum of the storm, and the challenges are both immediate and far-reaching. In the economic realm, as we have seen, the crucial task of the NIEs is to act in accordance with their comparative advantage as they climb up the technological ladder. They will be forerunners in the broad shift from a vertical to a horizontal division of labor in the regional and international arenas. To support this process, including the transferral of capital and technology, they must further reduce trade barriers, facilitate foreign investment, and provide greater protection for intellectual property rights. With most labor-intensive industries relocating to lower-income countries and certain capital-intensive industries rising in these societies, the NIEs have become a vital intermediate force, capable of contributing to the advances of those below them and of facilitating the adjustments of those above them.

The less-developed states within the authoritarian-pluralist category, and also those that can be defined as political democracies, must give priority to modifying their semi-autarkic, import-substitution, protectionist strategy in favor of an outward-looking strategy that promotes exports while facilitating the introduction of capital and technology. These states can be major suppliers of labor-intensive and certain skill-intensive products, while importing goods and components higher on the technological ladder and expanding their domestic market.

Admittedly, there are substantial psychological and political obstacles to greater regional and international integration. Nationalist counter-currents are inevitable, and they will be all the stronger because interest groups now have a greater voice in a more open political atmosphere. There is also a risk that, as in socialist states, powerful bureaucratic interests at the center or in key regions will effectively resist liberalization, freezing certain societies into economic immobility or, at a minimum, slowing the developmental process and causing it to deviate through a second economy.

One critically significant variable lies largely outside the control of Asia's NIEs and developing states. It consists in the policies—and the economic health—of the two Pacific-Asian economic superpowers, Japan and the United States. Can these two nations successfully deal with the structural changes already underway and destined to continue for the indefinite future? Will the macroeconomic policies implemented by these two governments serve the needs of their respective domestic economies, and at the same time those of the international community?

It is commonly acknowledged that major readjustments

are needed, particularly in the case of the United States. The principal uncertainty is whether the landing will be soft or hard, and what its effect upon others will be. In the case of Japan, an old culture clashes with new power, making internationalization a painful and incompletely consummated process. For both societies, the imperatives of interdependence and the increasing degree of economic integration still coexist uneasily with powerful nationalist impulses, the latter strengthened by the abuses that come with a highly competitive atmosphere and a lack of commonly accepted rules.

Even the formation of larger economic blocs via free-trade agreements will have an unpredictable influence on the broader thrust toward internationalization. Like the bilateral agreements that accompany—and sometimes impede—multilateral efforts, free-trade agreements represent a groping toward an international order, whose outcome is uncertain but which will inevitably alter prevailing concepts of national sovereignty as well as the economic practices that have been refined since the initial Industrial Revolution. The majority of Asian states—whether NIEs or less-developed countries—will be deeply affected by these developments without the ability to control or possibly to influence them.

With respect to political issues, the Asian authoritarian-pluralist states fall into two categories. Those now making the transition to competitive politics can be coupled with the older democracies. Those maintaining their former status will sooner or later face the question of how to go about instituting greater political openness, a course made increasingly probable by both their regional environment and their domestic socioeconomic development. Can such a transition take place gradually and with a minimum of violence, along a properly prepared path, or will such benefits be sacrificed and will change await some unexpected event or the erosion of public support, resulting in a possibly bloody uprising?

And once made, can the transition hold? Or, in the fashion

of certain Latin-American states, will there be seemingly endless pendulum swings between democratic and autocratic
rule, as democracy fails to solve problems sufficiently and
acquire legitimacy? It must be reiterated that while the main
current in Asia is presently running toward greater political
openness, the tides are not necessarily irreversible. Let me
turn now to the political issues that will confront Asian democracies in the years ahead.

With the exception of Sri Lanka, all of the Asian democratic states have so far nurtured a dominant-party system,
with one party or coalition continuously in power (India had
one short-term oppositionist government after Indira Gandhi's period of martial law, and South Korea currently has a
divided government). As I have noted, the dominant-party
system is moderated by the fact that other political forces
sometimes achieve control at regional levels. Nevertheless,
the accommodation of Asian democracy to periodic alterna-
tions of power at the center remains to be tested. When one
party knows only how to govern and others know only how
to oppose, none of them can be fully responsible.

A second, more fundamental issue bearing on democracy's
future in Asia—and elsewhere—relates to the racial, religious, and regional cleavages noted earlier. Irrespective of
political system, Asian societies have made little if any progress in race relations. In a number of countries, indeed, there
has been regression. The political role of religion, meanwhile,
has grown stronger in certain regions, and in some cases it is
a religion militant in its creed and tactics. Few if any social
scientists foretold the political role that fundamentalist reli-
gions would play in the world toward the close of the twentieth century. Perhaps we failed to appreciate the fact that in
a time of profound upheaval, when one's traditional lifestyle
and values are being assaulted and secular ideology has lost
much of its appeal, it is natural for people to turn to religion

as a source of emotional security and peace of mind. Sensing the opportunity or believing in the cause, leaders can then easily mold religion into a political movement, competitive with secularism and often divisive. If political choice merely exacerbates ethnic and religious cleavages, and if political appeals serve to heighten tensions, democracy is in jeopardy.

Regionalism has also shown great tenacity. The critical task for every state today is to extend governance simultaneously downward and outward. Capital-centered policies no longer suffice. To impose "imperial rule" while paying scant attention to local needs and problems is to court trouble. By decentralizing decision making, thereby strengthening local government while building a network that connects localities with each other in a common sense of nationhood, one gives the national government greater legitimacy, notwithstanding the special problems characteristic of greatly heterogeneous societies that undertake decentralization. At the same time, as I have emphasized, it is equally essential to enhance governance above the nation-state level, by instituting means for cooperative or integrated decision making across national boundaries. Such a development accords with the economic and political realities of our age.

A third variable in democracy's future, as I have repeatedly underlined, is that of leadership. The human factor was once relegated to a secondary position, not only by the historical determinists but also by those who thought that science and technology would reach a point where technicians could handle all administrative matters, and where governance would become a science instead of an art. They were wrong. In the contemporary world, as in the past, the average citizen turns to leaders to set the tone, explicate the issues, and bring institutions to life. In every society, politics remains in some degree personalized, and clearly this is true throughout Asia—now and for the foreseeable future. As noted, the inexperience of Corazon Aquino and Rajiv Gandhi, and their lack of skill in political management, both of their party and of their government, are matters of legitimate concern. In Malaysia at present, Datuk Seri Mahathir Mohamad, a confrontational leader, holds power after several decades during which the nation was led by consensus builders. This is having a negative influence on unity within the dominant party, within the government, and within Malaysia's precariously balanced racial groups. In Singapore, Lee Kuan Yew has announced that he will retire when he reaches sixty-five years of age. Perhaps this will give the younger politicians whom he has groomed opportunities to bring Singapore politics more in line with the new society that has emerged over the last three decades. Democracy depends upon constant reinvigoration, and one problem at the close of this century will be to find ways in which aged leaders can be peacefully removed from power.

The issues just raised lead to certain final reflections on the relationship between politics and development, and more specifically that relationship in twentieth-century Asia. Building upon experience accrued in previous eras, socioeconomic development in this century has centered upon these broad trends: economic diversification and expanded productivity through the application of science and technology to both agriculture and industry; rapidly growing populations, major increases in life expectancy, and rising urbanization; increased social mobility and a movement toward impersonal, rationalized social relationships; a greater capacity for mass mobilization through popular education, more sophisticated organizational techniques, and extraordinary advances in communications.

The political trends accompanying these developments are as follows: the emergence of the nation-state, armed with sovereignty, as the fountainhead of legitimate authority, and hence an increasing centralization of political power; the replacement of ascriptive officials with a more highly differentiated civil and military bureaucracy recruited through technical training and selected increasingly according to merit; the establishment of a comprehensive legal system founded on a national constitution, the standardization of law and legal procedures, the abolition of legally privileged classes, and a movement toward equal rights under the law for all citizens; and growing popular participation in the political process, albeit with radically different degrees of actual power granted to the public at large.

As we have seen, the evolution of Asian societies in these directions has varied greatly, despite the fact that Asian leaders have virtually all insisted on their dedication to these goals. Equally significant, the political strategies they have employed to achieve "modernization" in its twentieth-century forms have also varied greatly. The data make it abundantly clear that there has been very little correlation between political system and stage of socioeconomic development in modern Asia. The principal reason has been the availability of external values and institutional models. Latecomers did not have to—indeed, could not—follow "the natural course." Follower societies asked such questions as "Why can't we skip developmental stages, to catch up with the advanced world more quickly?" and "Why can't politics lead economic growth rather than merely be its reflection?"

This situation led to certain curious anomalies. Although some traditionalists saw modernization as Westernization and hence as a defilement of their culture and values, most Asian leaders made the commitment, believing that development in accordance with trends in the global stream could be harmonized with their own society's needs and nature. When it came to a political concept like democracy, however, many leaders, despite the extensive homage they paid to the principle, seriously doubted whether genuine freedom was compatible with rapid development. Thus, the Leninists appropriated the term "democracy" and demanded public participation in politics, but created a political system geared to conformity, trying to achieve unity through ideological exhortation, economic leveling, and guarantees of at least a minimal livelihood. And although this system had roots in the traditional societies in which it operated, in essence it was both modern and derived, since the words of Marx had been transformed and applied via Lenin to societies at the beginning rather than at the end of the developmental course.

On the whole, Leninist politics worked in the way in which it was intended, but its economics—and the culture it produced—were progressive failures. Today leaders are making an effort to put economics in command so that the stalled developmental process can go forward. Yet they continue to fear that if the natural political consequences of the new economic efforts are permitted to unfold freely, disunity and even chaos might result. Hence, the tension between the need for stability and the desire for political openness is certain to continue.

The imposition of parliamentary democracy upon certain late-developing Asian states was an even more unnatural action. A substantial number of failures ensued, but there have also been successes, despite socioeconomic conditions very different from those that have commonly been assumed necessary to nurture the democratic system. These societies managed to achieve and maintain elitist consensus, which led to sustained tutelage of the citizenry and hence to an overcoming of adverse social and economic conditions. To be sure, in virtually all of Asia's democracies the bureaucracy has played a powerful role, often dominating the policy-making process, and the dominant-party system has fostered stability. Moreover, long-term success unquestionably will depend upon progress in the economic and social fields.

The most natural strategy for the late-developing societies of twentieth-century Asia has been authoritarian-pluralism. Even this system was borrowed largely from external sources. By keeping a rein on political rights yet enabling initiatives to operate in such areas as enterprise and religion, governments achieved a mix of stability and dynamism suitable to indigenous conditions. It is thus not surprising that the Leninist states are now gravitating in this direction. Meanwhile, as we have seen, certain of the most successful authoritarian-pluralist societies have undertaken the transition to parliamentarism. Admittedly this is a hazardous step, since cultural change lags somewhat behind economic change—and in these societies cultural barriers to political openness abound. Nonetheless, experiment has the support of a majority of the political elites and also of the bulk of the new "middle classes" that have been its primary stimuli.

LET ME CONCLUDE on a positive note. Despite various unresolved problems, there are ample reasons for hope regarding Asia's future. The broad trends in economic policies and actions accord with the requirements of our times. The role of government, still vitally important, is generally being redirected to focus upon those spheres where its assistance or restraint is most needed. Nations are placing a higher premium on liberating the energy and creativity within the private sector, at a time when, through training and experience, this sector is generally better qualified to play an enhanced role in their societies. Although various forms of economic nationalism are still resilient and may be expected to mount new challenges in response to the trauma of rapid internationalization, virtually every nation now recognizes that the autarkic economy is outmoded; and all of them are seeking, in one way or another, to participate in the international division of labor. Thus, a growing transfer of skills and technology to the developing societies is underway, and economic regionalism of various types is coming into being, cutting across ideological-political lines.

One can discern other trends having far-reaching political implications. With a handful of exceptions, governments can no longer count on the blind allegiance of a people mobilized through ideological exhortation and sophisticated organization techniques. Nationalism remains a potent weapon, but the continued effectiveness even of this instrument hinges in some degree upon governmental performance in improving social and economic conditions. Like its economic counterpart, the autarkic polity has become obsolete. The people of virtually every nation are increasingly aware of developments in the world around them. The virus of progress is rapidly spreading.

It is thus not surprising that whether spawned by sweeping domestic advances or by external example, the drive for greater political openness and meaningful participation in the political process has expanded in diverse Asian societies. Some governments are responding cautiously, fearing that the stability essential to development will be adversely affected. Indeed, the recurrent appeals of stability and freedom will represent the great contrapuntal themes in the decades ahead. But the process of politicizing an ever larger proportion of the citizenry in a new, more substantive sense cannot be stopped or reversed for any considerable length of time. In all probability, a more complex, volatile politics is in the offing for many societies, but the dominant effect will be to enforce greater accountability on the part of government, and hence greater attention to the social and economic problems at hand.

These developments will naturally continue to influence international affairs. Relations between and among the major Pacific-Asian powers are more fluid today than at any time since World War II, but on balance the trend is toward a reduction of tension. As I have pointed out, each of these nations, as it confronts monumental domestic tasks, requires a foreign policy that will not interfere with the new priorities.

We are also faced with two seemingly contradictory but in reality eminently rational developments. On the one hand, given rapid growth in economic strength and a declining sense of external threat, a number of states are staking out more independent positions from those of the major power with which they have been allied. And the major powers in turn are no longer prepared to offer open-ended pledges of support. The nature of alliances is changing. At the same time, virtually every state is being drawn into an external economic orbit with political and strategic implications. Thus, nonalignment in its strict sense is increasingly less desirable and less possible.

There is another international trend that warrants attention. Although regionalism within Asia is still largely in embryonic form, ties among and between Asian states are proliferating, both at the subregional level and throughout the Pacific-Asian area as a whole. Witness the evolution of ASEAN, the South Pacific Forum, and SAARC (the South Asian Association for Regional Cooperation). Even in Northeast Asia, where historical factors and contemporary political divisions preclude regional organization, a soft regionalism has emerged, epitomized by the burgeoning economic ties that cut across ideological and political boundaries. This process can be described as Asianization, whereby states once foreign to each other and with minimal ties are intensifying their relations across a broad spectrum. Some aspects of Asianization are negative, rekindling traditional hostilities or engendering new controversies. But on balance, the growing interaction is positive, contributing both to economic development and to political openness. Nor are the two great Pacific powers, the United States and the Soviet Union (particularly the former), uninvolved in this process.

The decades ahead will bring new challenges. Already we can glimpse the future. The more affluent nations will shift their emphasis from the quantity to the quality of life, and will give increasing attention to vital environmental issues. In fact, all societies will have to cooperate in improving the environment, if future generations are to enjoy a fruitful life. This agenda is full, including issues ranging from population planning to clean air and water.

Our planet is shrinking and our universe is expanding, signaling another set of important issues for the years ahead. In the political realm, all nations will increasingly turn their attention to strengthening governance and ties at the community level, where the citizen's daily life and concerns weigh so heavily. And that will include attention to fortifying the family, which has been so adversely affected by certain aspects of modernization. Meanwhile, at the regional and international levels, nations will be preoccupied with the construction of new institutions and attitudes compatible with the growth of economic interdependence. The demands of nationalism and internationalism will have to be balanced, and in some degree, blended. At the same time, as we move further into the space age, entirely new issues relating to politics and economics will unfold.

One can also be certain that the quest for values will continue. Indeed, it is very likely that such a quest will intensify, since pragmatism and relativism—the dominant trends of the present—can never be completely satisfying to the great majority of people. Further scientific advances in such fields as genetics will raise new and profound moral and ethical questions. The prolongation of life will also pose social and moral issues, whose dimensions we are only beginning to grasp. An extraordinary era lies ahead.

The nineteenth century has aptly been described as a time when Western intellectuals, with a few exceptions, were united in their boundless optimism about the future. The twentieth century provided ample ground for pessimists, some of them of the apocalyptic school. The early signs suggest that as we enter the twenty-first century, we should be cautiously optimistic and at the same time wary of all final solutions.

Index